ABOUT NICOLA MORGAN

Nicola Morgan is an international expert in stress, well-being and learning. She has written many books, including *Blame My Brain: The Amazing Teenage Brain Revealed*, *The Teenage Guides to Stress, Friends* and *Life Online*, *Positively Teenage* and *Body Brilliant*, and won numerous awards including the School Library Association's Outstanding Contribution award.

After learning the hard way how to manage her own well-being, Nicola now practises what she teaches, valuing sleep, food, exercise and relaxation, even when her workload looks overwhelming. Her mission is to use what she has learnt about the brain and stress management to empower young people to be the active agents in their own health and success.

Nicola's website has masses of information for families, schools, professionals and individual young people: www.nicolamorgan.com.

Follow Nicola on Twitter: @nicolamorgan

Author website: www.nicolamorgan.com

POSITIVE GUIDE TO
EXP... ...G STRESS

First published in Great Britain in 2020 by The Watts Publishing Group
Text copyright © Nicola Morgan 2020
Cover and inside design copyright © Franklin Watts 2020

10 9 8 7 6 5 4 3 2 1

Managing editor: Victoria Brooker
Inside design: Rocket Design (East Anglia) Ltd
Inside illustrations: Shutterstock
Consultant: Helen Keevil, Assistant Head (Pupil Welfare) at Epsom College

ISBN: 978 1 4451 7041 1 (pbk)
ISBN: 978 1 4451 7103 6 (e-book)

Printed and bound in Great Britain by Clays Ltd, Elcograf S.p.A.

Franklin Watts
An imprint of
Hachette Children's Group
Part of The Watts Publishing Group
Carmelite House
50 Victoria Embankment
London EC4Y 0DZ
An Hachette UK Company
www.hachette.co.uk
www.franklinwatts.co.uk

Shutterstock: Sukarno Achmad 14t; Alexzel 11,60b; Aluna1 73t; Arkadivna 35,54,
58,117t; Rashad Ashur 69b; handini_atmodiwiryo 95b; AVA Bitter 84,120c;
BenitoDesign 41; Bioraven 52; Nipatsara Bureepia 123; Creative icon styles 138c;
cubicidea 10; Elena35667 119c; Gazoukoo 55t; Alena Hovorkova 110t; Hudhud94
36; Farid Huseynov 72; Illustratioz 141b; Jemastock 85, 107c; Marta Jonina 111t;
Anastasios Kandris 16; Yevgen Kravchenko 29; Lia Li 108t; Lineartestpilot 20;
Lumpenmoiser 18; Megavectors 134b; MicroOne 57b,103b; Sasha Mosyagina 86;
Muuraa 87; Adrian Niederhaeuser 14b; lena_nikilaeva 125b; Oke 112b; Okili77 136b;
123Done 128; Alexander_P 89; Natasha Pankina 12; PavloS 56, 117b; Pranch 47; Arak
Rattanawijittakorn 15; Viktorija Reuta 6; Serhiy Smirnov 7; TopVectorElements 78, 102;
Visual Generation 77; pear worapan 69t; Ekaterina Zimodro 103t.
p93 © Katherine Lynas

Every attempt has been made to clear copyright. Should there be any inadvertent
omission please apply to the publisher for rectification.

The website addresses (URLs) included in this book were valid at the time of going to
press. However, it is possible that contents or addresses may have changed since the
publication of this book. No responsibility for any such changes can be accepted by
either the author or the Publisher.

Contents

INTRODUCTION

**Exams are stressful and most people don't love them! The
good news is that some stress improves performance. But
I can help you control it, so you avoid problems and have
the greatest chance of doing your best.**

Exam Attack is about more than managing stress, though.
It covers the latest discoveries about the science of learning
techniques – and these can really help you.

It's also about essential well-being.
Well-being directly affects performance. It's
not an optional luxury but how we give our
brain and body the best chance of success.

So, *Exam Attack* shows you how to manage
stress, learn effectively and prepare your
brain and body to be super-fit for exams!

I follow my own advice, too! I am naturally
anxious and my work involves tough
deadlines and public speaking. Exams are
like public speaking: preparation; nerves;
winding down afterwards and winding up to do
it again. I often speak on different topics one after
the other, so I must allocate enough time for each. I have to plan
carefully and manage energy levels, sleep and appetite problems.

That's a lot like facing exams.

I also have experience (like most people) of not doing as well as I wanted in exams. But exams are only one step to a destination and there are lots of ways of being successful in life without great school results. In fact, look at high-achieving people and you'll find that school exam success doesn't feature for many. Sometimes, we learn more from not getting top grades: it makes us try harder, think differently, be more determined. And those are important for a successful life.

But, of course, you want to get the best grades you can, because you'll feel good and because exams do open doors and smooth paths. That's what *Exam Attack* is for: to help you get through as successfully and smoothly as possible. It will give you the tools to control your body and mind during this challenging phase. And the tools will help you at many other stressful times of life. These are the sort of skills that employers are always looking for.

You'll find advice on food (and how to cope when you lose your appetite), sleep, panic, revision, getting help, managing screens and social media. And there's up-to-date advice on note-taking and learning. Take on board as much as you can and feel yourself gradually gain control.

WHEN SHOULD YOU READ EXAM ATTACK?

Ideally, several months before exams. Then come back to it nearer the time. Some of the advice is best followed well in advance and some is designed to help you on the day. But don't worry if you don't have much time left: there are many strategies that can be started quite close to exams.

ACTION!

As you're reading *Exam Attack*, some of the advice will feel especially important or useful for you. You might think you'll remember but the way to be sure – and the best way not to overload your busy brain – is to jot down the most important points somewhere, including page references. Then, if you're having a day when it's hard to be motivated to study, refer to your list and reread sections to help get you in the revision mindset and spur you into action once again.

SECTION I
THE RIGHT MINDSET

This section is all about your mental attitude. It will grow your confidence, as you discover that you have the power to affect your results.

It's equally important whether you're someone who finds schoolwork easy or not; whether your ambitions are high or more modest; whether in the past you've succeeded often or struggled.

IMAGINE YOU'RE AN ATHLETE

If you were a top athlete approaching a competition, your coach would not *only* focus on the skills for your sport. A coach would create a programme that included:

▶ Self-belief and a positive attitude

▶ Managing stress

▶ A planned timetable of training

▶ Nutrition

▶ Hydration

▶ Sleep

▶ Relaxation

▶ Dealing with setbacks

▶ Asking for help

- ▶ Growth mindset – the belief that hard work is how we become skilled
- ▶ *How* to practise
- ▶ What competition day will feel like; what will happen
- ▶ Stamina
- ▶ Preventing and dealing with injury or illness
- ▶ Dealing with disappointment

Exams are just like a sporting competition and you are the athlete. Meet your exam coach: me! Through *Exam Attack*, I will coach you as you approach your big day, so that you produce your best performance. We will cover everything on that list.

You're going to be so exam-ready!

As with sport, there are things we can't control: the questions you'll get, for example. Also, exam grade boundaries are often adjusted according to the overall performance of students that year. You can't completely control things, such as feeling ill or events going on in your life, that might not be related to exams. What this book will do is give you the best chance of being at peak performance and so the best chance of success. No guarantees, but improved chances.

Let's get started!

GROWTH MINDSET -
LEARNING BY DOING

People used to believe talents were simply things we were born with: we were either going to be good at something or we weren't. Now we know that we become expert at things far more through good teaching followed by practice and determination, rather than through 'talents' we were born with.

A 'GROWTH MINDSET' IS A WAY OF THINKING THAT SAYS 'I WILL LEARN NEW SKILLS AND BECOME BETTER AT THEM THROUGH MY OWN EFFORTS, ACTIONS AND DETERMINATION.'

The opposite of this, a 'fixed mindset', is a way of thinking that says, 'I just don't have the skills to be good at this, so no matter how hard I try I'll never master it.' The more you can do to build a growth mindset for yourself, the more you will feel empowered. You'll also be able to allow yourself to take small steps towards your goal, rather than giving up at the start because the goal looks impossible.

However, we need to recognise that some people are also born with advantages: perhaps not inborn talents but childhood experiences and opportunities, meaning they 'practise' certain skills from a young age. Imagine your parents are an engineer and a writer; imagine they're both keen to share their passions and skills. They bought you a construction kit and praised what you built; you were motivated to create even better constructions; your engineer parent showed (taught) you how force and motion work. Your writer parent praised your early reading and writing, sharing books and word games. Both parents loved seeing you develop skills and confidence. You went to science museums and libraries while your parents shared their enthusiasm *and* explained everything to you. They were teaching and you were practising, although it seemed like play.

You started school more advanced in those areas than some classmates. But some classmates had more exposure to painting, or sport, or swimming, or musical instruments. They seemed 'talented' at those things. You seemed 'talented' at the things you were good at. But you were all only good at those things because:

1 You had loads of teaching even if you didn't notice.

2 You're genuinely interested and like these activities (because young children imitate their parents and because you enjoyed praise).

3 You've been practising even though it didn't feel like practising.

As an example, a child who reads for 20 minutes a day every school day for the first six years of school – which children who love reading will do – will have read (practised reading) for just over 60 school days by the end of primary school. A child who has only read for five minutes a day – because they didn't really like it so just did it when they had to – will only have read for 12 school days. Which one will be likely to be a 'better', more confident reader and know more words? So, not cleverer or more talented at reading: they just practised more because they liked it more.[1] Children who also read at weekends and in holidays will have even more hours of practice.

A 'GROWTH MINDSET' MEANS BELIEVING THAT WHEN WE PRACTISE AND WORK HARD AT SOMETHING WE GET BETTER. THIS PUTS POWER IN YOUR HANDS INSTEAD OF THE HANDS OF CHANCE.

There's more about this in 'Practice and your brain' on page 56.

ACTION!

Think of something you can do better than you could a year ago. Write a note to congratulate yourself for working so hard. You made that happen.

★ ★ ★ IN SHORT ★ ★ ★

Everything you can do, you can only do because you practised it. Anything you want to do better will happen if you persevere. You need to start with the right teaching but then it's down to you: listen, understand, revisit, practice.

....

1   Based on 190 days of school in a year and a school day of 09.00-15.00

STRESS - DON'T FEAR IT

We usually talk about stress negatively. 'I feel so stressed', 'He's off work with stress', 'That's caused by stress.' There are whole websites, organisations and books – including mine! – devoted to teaching people how to reduce it.

Let's look at what stress actually is.

When I was about 13, I was chased by a goose. Don't laugh: geese are aggressive, fast, and can deliver a painful bite. I did the sensible thing: I ran. Very fast – far faster than I normally could – and vaulted a huge gate. Safe on the other side, I wondered how I could possibly have jumped that high or even dared try.

Now I understand how: stress. It's a response evolved in early humans (and other animals) to keep us safe from attacks, whether by lions, snakes or enemies. When the brain detects any threat, it instantly triggers hormones – mainly adrenaline and cortisol – through the body, creating many immediate changes and making us ready to act in whatever way might be necessary.

The most obvious effects of these chemicals are to speed heart-rate and breathing, taking blood *away* from where it's not likely to be needed (skin, for example) and to where it may be needed (large muscles). Another noticeable effect is that we focus our attention intensely on the threat, with the result that we often don't notice other things, sometimes even pain.

This is sometimes called the 'fight, flight or freeze' response. Our brain instantly makes us ready either to fight against an enemy, run away super-fast or freeze so that our enemy doesn't see us. To get a sense of how quickly

it works, think about when you jump in shock. Your physical reaction comes before the thinking parts of your brain interpret the actual situation.

We tend to talk about adrenaline but you'll also hear of noradrenaline, which is closely linked but different in complex ways. You may also hear of epinephrine and norepinephrine: these are alternative words for adrenaline and noradrenaline. Adrenaline and cortisol act together in many ways to create the stress response that we experience.

So, stress evolved to keep early humans safe by helping them run extra fast, fight extra hard or be extra strong. But what does this have to do with our lives now? After all, genuinely life-threatening situations such as being chased by a predator are rare.

This is where we need to understand the word 'threat'.

A THREAT MIGHT NOT BE PHYSICAL. IT MIGHT BE A MENTAL CHALLENGE.

It might be meeting a stranger, speaking in public, being watched or judged. A threat is anything, big or small, which requires us to react in some way. It can even be a negative thought, or something imaginary. For example, 'I have exams soon.' Or 'What if I get cancer?'

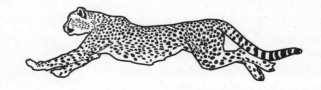

At the instant of the stress response, the brain hasn't had time to work out *what* the stress is. (This is why we jump at the sound of a bang, before immediately realising that it was just a car backfiring or a door banging.) The brain triggers our super-performance, just in case.

Our daily lives are full of occurrences which trigger stress responses. They can be things that dominate the mind and are impossible to ignore, such as a medical symptom, worrying about parental break-up or being bullied, or smaller events, such as realising you've done the wrong homework, being asked to speak up in class, or having to deal with a nasty comment.

ONE THING THAT TRIGGERS A STRESS RESPONSE IS CRITICISM.

That makes sense when you think about how you feel when you're criticised. You feel threatened. You *are* threatened, through your self-esteem. So, when an adult says something that makes you feel your work isn't good enough or suggests that you're not on course for passing an exam, your body interprets this as stress, a threat to you, something you have to react to.

These events trigger the stress chemicals in our bodies each time, raising our heart rate and making us alert, tense. That's why stress can be such a negative thing nowadays: modern life brings more (but usually less life-threatening) stresses than for ancient humans.

That's what stress *is*. But what practical problems does it cause?

Stress can be a problem in three main ways:

1 **The adrenaline problem.** This can take two forms:

▶ Too much – we feel panicky, so it's hard to do our best. It can also become a panic attack (see page 126).

▶ Wrong time – we might feel anxious when we don't need to. For example, feeling anxious as you walk towards an exam and turn the paper over should help you perform, but feeling anxious when trying to sleep or relax isn't useful.

2 **The cortisol problem.** Cortisol takes longer to disappear from our system than adrenaline. If you have lots of stresses during the day, cortisol builds up. This will cause problems with sleep, mood, concentration, self-control and your immune system. Because some of these problems might not appear immediately, people often don't realise they're stress-related.

3 **Brain bandwidth over-occupation.** There's something we talk about called 'attention span' or 'brain bandwidth': how many things we can focus on or do at one time. Our attention works a bit like broadband or wifi bandwidth or even a computer processor: we only have a fixed amount of 'bandwidth' or 'processing power' so if a lot of our brain's attention is occupied by certain actions, it becomes harder or impossible to do other actions or do them well. We have a fixed amount of 'bandwidth' and everything we consciously do occupies part of it.

Some things occupy a little bandwidth (typically things that are easy or familiar, such as walking or wiggling your fingers or counting from 1 to 10) and others occupy a lot (things that are difficult or unfamiliar, such as learning a new dance routine or piece of music, reading something difficult, or working out 17 + 158 + 49.) When we have too much 'on our mind', we struggle to find bandwidth to focus on our work, for example. It *feels* stressful, unpleasant, overwhelming. We might cope for a while but soon we need a break. You'll have experienced the feeling of being overwhelmed by information, instructions, noise, things you've got to do, two people talking to you at once. That's brain bandwidth overload.

Try listening to two people talking at once and you'll find you can't take in what they're both saying. This is because listening to the human voice typically occupies over half your brain bandwidth.

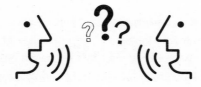

One thing that takes up a *lot* of bandwidth is worry: so, if you have something major on your mind, you'll find it harder to divert your attention to a task such as school work.

I will show you strategies to stop these negative stress effects becoming a problem and to allow stress to do what it's there for – super-performance – rather than become a negative force. You'll find the strategies in the section on Relaxation (see page 115), specifically:

▶ To solve the adrenaline problem and feelings of panic you'll need the breathing and relaxation exercises on pages 124–126.

▶ To solve or avoid cortisol build-up, you'll need to inject relaxation activities into your day, such as these on pages 116–119.

▶ Solutions for preoccupation and negative thoughts, having too much 'on your mind', are on pages 117–118.

You need all of these strategies if you're to have the best control over your stress and the best well-being. And it's much better to learn about them and practise *before you need them.*

THESE STRATEGIES ARE NOT JUST FOR EXAMS BUT FOR YOUR WHOLE LIFE.

Your adults will benefit from them, too!

★ ★ ★ IN SHORT ★ ★ ★

Stress is natural and has evolved to make you super-perform. But you need to keep it in control so as to avoid it creating poor health and reducing performance. Luckily, the strategies for this are tried and tested and not complicated. You can be in control of your stress and that control will help you perform at your best.

THE IMPORTANCE OF WELL-BEING

Well-being is not a soft optional extra or luxury. It will affect your performance, whatever gender, age, background or education.

WELL-BEING IS A STATE OF BODY AND MIND WHICH MEANS YOU HAVE A STRONG FOUNDATION OF PHYSICAL AND MENTAL HEALTH.

It gives you the best chance of succeeding at whatever you're trying to do.

Well-being doesn't change quickly. With good well-being, you could catch a minor virus or have an emotional upset, but your well-being would remain strong. However, if too many negative things happened and you hadn't had a chance to top up your reserves (see page 93), you would notice it diminish.

I talk about a 'well of well-being'. If yours is full, you can afford to lose some – during a stressful period such as exams, for example. But you have to keep topping it up or eventually it will run dry. If your well isn't very full to start with, it will be drained more quickly.

WELL-BEING GIVES YOU RESILIENCE: THE ABILITY TO BOUNCE BACK AFTER SOMETHING BAD OR DIFFICULT.

It gives you perspective: you had a bad day, or were ill, or perhaps failed in some way, but you can pick yourself up and try again. It gives you optimism: today is tough and this feels bad but tomorrow or next week or next month can be better. 'I've been well and strong before and I will be so again.'

I can do this.

_____

WELL-BEING IS NOT SOMETHING YOU'RE BORN WITH. IT'S SOMETHING YOU BUILD UP, WITH SMALL POSITIVE ACTIONS.

_____

You might need help – and that's what I'm here for. Some people need more help than others, perhaps if they lack support from people around them, or their life contains tougher challenges. But everyone *can* have better well-being.

Your well-being is at the heart of my thinking as your exam coach. Happily, there are loads of ways to build it. Simple, tested ways, which aren't difficult! In fact, most are enjoyable and fun. You'll feel great.

Well-being advice runs through this book but the most practical section is SECTION FOUR on page 93.

★ ★ ★ **IN SHORT** ★ ★ ★

Well-being is not a luxury. It helps you be successful and achieve more of your goals. Feeling better is the foundation of doing better. Don't ignore it and don't let it wait till after exams: you need it now!

DIFFERENT CHALLENGES

You are all different, all with a variety of personalities, conditions and home lives. You might be too stressed or not stressed enough; you might just need help in one area. And not everyone has the same support at home or a comfortable, quiet place to work from.

PERSONALITY AND EXAMS

I never suggest trying to change underlying personality but there are traits which can have a negative effect on how we feel and perform. It's worth seeing how we can moderate some of our unhelpful behaviours.

Type A or Type B personality?

One personality division, dating from the 1950s, categorises us as 'Type A' or 'Type B'. Some people are strongly one or the other, while others may be less easy to categorise. See whether you recognise yourself in one of these descriptions.

Type A people tend to be ambitious, driven, impatient, serious and in a hurry to get anywhere; they often cope badly with failure and drive themselves hard. They get irritated easily, especially by people messing around or not taking life seriously. They tend to be worriers and overthinkers. Some of these behaviours improve exam performance, such as working hard, and others hinder performance because Type As may not relax enough.

? *If you think you are a Type A personality:*

▶ Pay extra attention to my advice on looking after yourself and particularly on relaxation (see page 115).

▶ You may have difficulty sleeping, so take note of those sections, too (see pages 106–115).

▶ Look out for (and then avoid) unhealthy behaviours such as working late at night, getting up very early, missing meals or avoiding friends.

▶ When something goes wrong, be your own best friend: treat yourself as you would a friend who has just had a bad day.

▶ A stress-buddy could be really useful for you (see page 61).

Type B people tend to be more laidback. They don't worry too much or overthink. They don't rush about or overburden their workload and they are more patient with other people and themselves. Some of these behaviours improve performance, protecting them from stress-related illness, and others hinder, because they might not be motivated to work hard enough or early enough.

? *If you think you are a Type B personality:*

▶ If you lack motivation or leave your work too late, pay special attention to the sections on goals, planning and schedules.

▶ Even though you seem more laid-back, you can be just as vulnerable to low self-esteem, which might happen when you feel yourself getting behind. Ask a teacher or other adult to help you create a schedule that keeps you motivated and on track.

▶ Could you set more ambitious goals and targets (see pages 90–92)?

▶ A revision partner (see page 63) could be really useful for you.

ACTION!

Do you completely lack motivation and feel like not getting out of bed because there's no point? Please talk to an adult and perhaps see your GP. This can be a sign of a form of depression. Or there could be some simple underlying reason that a doctor or other adult could spot and solve.

A PERFECTIONIST PERSONALITY

Many *Type A* people also have perfectionist tendencies. Perfectionists find it hard to be satisfied with anything less than the best and will focus on what they didn't achieve, rather than what they did.

Being ambitious is good because you'll set high targets and often achieve them. But the downside is that when you don't achieve your goals, it will affect you worse than someone with a more laid-back personality. Even if it's not your fault that you didn't do well, you may still blame yourself. Perfectionists fret for too long about what went wrong rather than picking themselves up and trying again.

Fear of failure might stop a perfectionist from trying. Self-esteem can drop and opportunities may be missed.

How to deal with perfectionist tendencies

▶ Speak to yourself with the voice of a friend who cares. What would this friend say? Probably that no one's perfect; you're doing really well; everyone makes mistakes; mistakes are there to learn from; failing at first will make eventual success feel even better when it comes.

▶ Take extra care of your stress and energy levels by doing all my relaxation tips later in the book.

▶ Make your goals high but not too high. See page 90–92 for how to set SMART goals.

▶ Praise someone else – it will make you and them feel better.

Lack of confidence

Both *Type A* and *Type B* people can lack confidence: it's not a personality type but more of a mindset.

Very ambitious and successful people can be surprisingly unconfident. You might be doing really well at school but still fear that this is some kind of illusion, that it's all luck and one day the luck will run out. Your parents might praise you but you think, 'They're just saying that because they're my parents.' This is 'imposter syndrome', when people believe their success is based on illusion or luck and that one day it will tumble down.

Seemingly laidback *Type B* behaviour is sometimes a cover for lack of confidence: 'I can't do that so I won't try.' *Type Bs* might pretend they don't mind while minding very much underneath.

How to deal with lack of confidence

▶ First, analyse. Is it just about exams or more? The answer will help you know who to talk to.

▶ Talk to an adult who knows you well. This need not be your parent or carer, but maybe a family friend or a club leader.

▶ Share your feelings with a friend. Make clear that you aren't 'fishing for compliments' but you want strategies for feeling better about yourself.

▶ Remind yourself that confidence levels change, depending on what's going on. So, this could be temporary.

▶ Perhaps you have been setting targets which are too high – or had them set for you by someone who pushed too far. Can you lower the targets?

▶ Make a list of things you are good at and things you've achieved. Remind yourself that you *can* do things well and no one can do everything well.

▶ Spend time each day doing something that makes you feel good about yourself and with people who boost your confidence, not drag you down.

Understanding what type of person you are can help you know what your pressure points might be in the lead-up to exams, whether you'll be a worrier or more laidback, and how motivation and confidence might be strengths or challenges. This can help you keep on the right track and ask for tailored help.

NEURODIVERSITY AND EXAMS – LEARNING DIFFERENCES

No two brains are the same but there are certain typical patterns. When we use the term 'neurodiverse' to describe people with a wide range of very different conditions, such as dyslexia, autism, ADHD or dyspraxia, we're saying that these are variations on how human brains are most often wired. Neurodiverse people may do lots of things the same as other people but other things differently or with more difficulty. It is not to do with intelligence: many neurodiverse people can do extraordinary things that make them seem super-clever but may have great difficulties with skills that neurotypical people learn easily.

Some people use the term 'specific learning difficulties'. Certainly neurodiverse people often have difficulties but these conditions are *not* always negative. In exams, neurodiverse people often do face specific challenges. Schools and parents or carers need to understand those challenges so that neurodiverse people can get help to compete on a more level playing-field.

If you have one or more of the conditions below, I hope you're already getting the right kind of help and that your adults have a good understanding not only of your variation but also your individual needs within that (because two people with the same condition will not be the same).

Unfortunately, many people are diagnosed later than ideal. If you've only recently been identified, the adults supporting you may not understand how best to help. For example, people often think dyslexia is just about reading, writing and spelling, whereas it affects many other skills, such as organisation, planning and memory.

THE ADVICE THAT FOLLOWS IS AIMED AT BOTH YOU AND YOUR SUPPORTING ADULTS. SHOW IT TO THEM!

---

*The approaches are different in different countries but in progressive education and social systems there is good support for neurodiverse people, often including extra time in exams or tools which other students aren't allowed. These do not provide an advantage: they offer a fairer starting point. **NOTE:** Many neurodiverse conditions overlap and some people will have elements of several. Also, whichever you have, all the general advice later in the book also applies.*

DYSLEXIA

Dyslexia is a well-known set of learning difficulties and ranges from mild to severe, often running in families. Dyslexia has nothing to do with intelligence and many very successful, creative and high-achieving people have this condition.

EVERYONE WILL EXPERIENCE DYSLEXIA DIFFERENTLY AND THERE ARE POSITIVE AND NEGATIVE ASPECTS.

Positives can include powerful creative abilities, being able to think 'outside the box', noticing patterns or details that others don't, having interesting ways of problem-solving. Typical negatives can include problems with specific aspects of reading, writing, remembering sequences and instructions, memory, organisation and planning.

The difficulties are *specific rather than general*. So, a person with dyslexia might be really good at remembering some things but unexpectedly poor at remembering others. They might be good at reading to themselves but not at reading aloud. They might be able to remember facts and speak articulately on a topic but not be able to write the points down coherently. Their hand-writing might be illegible but their artwork brilliant.

There can also be problems with processing information, whether information that you've heard or that you've read. Many people with dyslexia, when hearing an instruction with more than one part, will miss the second part because they're still processing the first.

DYSCALCULIA

Dyscalculia is closely connected to dyslexia except that the core difficulties are with numbers and mathematical concepts rather than written words. It's common to have both. Skills such as telling the time, remembering sequences, remembering mathematical processes and planning ahead are often affected.

DYSGRAPHIA

Many people with dyslexia and/or dyscalculia also have dysgraphia, a specific difficulty with writing. People may have difficulties with hand-writing, typing, spelling, forming letters and organising thoughts onto paper. You can have either without the other.

A common feature of all these conditions is difficulty with organisation, time-tabling and planning ahead. That's partly why exams can bring enormous extra stress.

Advice for exam students with dyslexia, dyscalculia and dysgraphia:

1 Make sure all the adults in your life (home and school) realise that planning might be difficult and that your difficulties do not come from lack of effort. You need a) help and b) strategies and aids, not nagging. You'll probably need help with revision timetables.

2 Make sure your school uses any provisions allowed, such as extra time and a laptop. Someone might be allowed to read the questions and even write your dictated answers. For this, your school must organise an official assessment in advance.

3 It's extra important to be very familiar with what to expect in the exam. Lots of people mis-read instructions – such as how many questions to answer – and the more practice you can have in advance the better.

4 As dyslexia (etc) often runs in families, it's possible that the adults you live with may have some of the same problems as you. This can be helpful, because they will be able to empathise, but they may also struggle to read the questions or plan ahead. So find an adult who is confident about this.

5 Use the same revision techniques as for short-term memory problems (see page 37).

6 'To-do' lists and charts mean you don't have to hold so much in your head, freeing your brain for actual learning.

7 Routines also free up brain space. For example, create a routine of always putting tomorrow's school stuff neatly by your door each evening.

8 If you have dysgraphia, experiment with different writing implements as some are much easier to write neatly with than others. Make sure you have several spares of your favourites.

HOLD ON TO THIS IDEA:
EACH SPECIFIC LEARNING DIFFICULTY IS MORE OF A PROBLEM AT SCHOOL THAN IT WILL BE LATER.

As an adult, there will be huge opportunities for you. Neurodiverse people have many strengths and talents not tested in exams.

Your chance will come!

DYSPRAXIA

Although someone with dyslexia or dyscalculia might also have dyspraxia, it is a very different condition.

Dyspraxia is also known as developmental co-ordination disorder (DCD) and problems with co-ordination are the most obvious symptoms. Many of the things we do as humans need very detailed movements of our fingers and 'hand-eye co-ordination'. This affects actions such as tying shoelaces, handling cutlery and using implements to write or draw. The handwriting of someone with dyspraxia can be very hard to read.

Memory and planning are often affected; it may be difficult to acquire sporting skills and some people will find reading difficult because it involves controlling eye movement.

It is a set of difficulties that can bring a wide range of problems throughout life, and each individual will need different help.

Advice for exam students with dyspraxia:

▶ As with dyslexia, make sure you have a trusted adult who knows your exact condition and can be your advocate.

▶ Get to know as much as you can about your specific difficulties, so you can be your own expert. Perhaps identify your main 3–5 problems and discuss them with your trusted adult. Then you can discuss possible ways to tackle those problems. It might be a special strategy, a tool such as a whiteboard in your room, a relaxation technique, or speaking to a particular teacher at school.

▶ Follow all the guidance for dyslexia, above.

THE AUTISTIC SPECTRUM

Autism includes an enormous range of individual experiences, from relatively mild to very severe. The phrase 'on the spectrum' is sometimes used to describe someone on this range. One of the best-known typical features of autism is a difficulty in 'reading the minds' of other people and so in communicating, but some individuals with autism have immense talents alongside their difficulty in social skills, while others are extremely disabled. People with autism tend to have a different way of thinking from others and it's often a very clear, creative and powerful way of thinking.

Asperger syndrome is generally considered part of the autistic spectrum. It's characterised by average or above average intelligence and usually no language delay. It's often described as 'high-functioning autism' because it's less disabling.

Many people on the spectrum, including those with Asperger's, also have mental health problems.

What does this mean for exams?
People on the spectrum can do extremely well in exams because when they know what the task is they are often incredibly focused, engaged and determined to learn. Their memory skills are often excellent and they can do particularly well in sciences and maths.

Another common feature is the need for routine, familiarity and controlled settings. People with autism often become extremely uncomfortable and distressed when things are unfamiliar or unexpected. This can make it virtually impossible to perform well; they may need to leave the room.

Find an adult to act as your advocate. Get your adult to read my advice with you and help you work out what applies to you, creating a personal action plan, which you can share with school.

Advice for exam students with autism:

I have broken these into topics to make them clearer.

Getting help early and planning ahead

▶ Make sure that an adult who understands can advocate for you. This may involve a meeting with teachers. If face-to-face meetings are difficult, then send an email or a letter. Keep this adult informed about your worries. If you don't tell them, they won't know.

▶ Make a list of things that are essential for your concentration and ensure relevant adults do anything possible to make them happen. Possibilities: a certain type of chair; a specific pen or pencil case; sitting in a particular place in the room. You know what you need: ask for it and explain why it's important. Sometimes, you just can't have what you ask for; discuss how you will cope.

▶ Would it help if you could do exams in a separate room? It might be impossible or you might need to be with a few other students but it's worth asking.

▶ Will a trusted adult who knows your needs be accessible on the day? What happens if that adult is ill or called away?

▶ If you take any medication, make sure you have everything you need.

Knowing what to expect

▶ Ask to familiarise yourself with the exam room well in advance.

▶ Find out the rules in advance: what you can ask and what you can't; what to do if you need the toilet; what you're allowed and not allowed to have with you.

▶ Find out what will happen from the moment you arrive, so there are no surprises. Practise in your head or role-play.

▶ If someone will be reading questions to you, make sure you know what you can and can't ask that person to do.

▶ Will there be a room where you can go if stressed out?

▶ If noises distract you, would earplugs or headphones help? Or can a noisy machine be turned off? Discuss with your trusted adult.

▶ If you use 'feelings cards' to express emotions, check that you'll be able to use them during the exam.

▶ Do you have calming strategies to help if you feel panicky? You will find examples on pages 125–127. Practise in advance.

▶ Remember that most people feel anxious about exams. Some might be feeling worse than you!

▶ Often people with autism have perfectionist tendencies and think they have to get everything right: you don't!

▶ Revising is not cheating: it's practising. It's how we learn things. Revision is part of learning; it makes information go into long-term memory.

▶ Remember: exams aren't the most important thing in the world but you are very smart and, if you don't write anything down, people won't know how smart you are!

MEMORY PROBLEMS

There are many sorts of memory and various theories about how memory works. There's a lot we don't yet know. Most people would like their memory to be better, that's for sure. But some people will have more problems than others with learning and retaining new information and recalling it later. And that obviously affects exams.

You'll hear people talk about short-term and long-term memory. Short-term memory generally refers to when we hold some information in our mind for a few seconds while we use it. For example, some figures that we're adding up. We use long term memory to hold some information for much longer. And we usually have to make an effort for that to happen – though sometimes it happens with little effort.

I'll be covering many of the tricks about learning later in the book, but for now I want to mention very briefly some advice for people with a medical reason for memory problems. A 15-year-old girl emailed me and I thought her question was useful and interesting. It's a great example of a young person really understanding and respecting her neurodiversity and taking steps to make her brain work well for her.

'Hi Nicola,

'I am 15 years old and I have a brain injury causing short-term memory loss. I have 3 science exams on the 11th, 12th and 13th of May and I was just wondering if you had any tips on how to revise?'

On the next page is the outline of the advice I gave her and it will work very well for many of you.

Advice for exam students with memory problems:

▶ Follow the learning tips in Section Three – they will all work for you just as well as for anyone else.

▶ Especially follow the advice about engaging as many senses as possible (see page 38).

▶ Focus on understanding something before trying to remember it. So, try explaining it in your own words before you try to commit it to memory.

▶ Set shorter periods for concentration – 20 minutes at a time. Take a break after each one.

20 min

▶ Try to learn one thing at a time. Get that straight before you add another one. Don't overload your brain or you'll remember nothing.

▶ When you get into the exam, quickly write down things you particularly want to remember. Make sure you do this on paper provided in the exam.

▶ Short-term memory is negatively affected by stress, so take care of your stress levels.

▶ A brilliant game for improving memory is 'I went to the shops'. It involves starting with, 'I went to the shops and I bought a cat' (for example). The next person says, 'I went to the shops and bought a cat and...' and adds something else etc. This is a useful memory exercise on its own but you could adapt it to learn words or facts for your revision, for example by 'shopping' for French vocab, mathematical formula, chemical compounds, historical dates, names of parts of the heart.

ATTENTION DEFICIT HYPERACTIVITY DISORDER

Usually called ADHD or ADD (attention deficit disorder), this involves great difficulty in concentrating, sitting still, and self-control. It is harder to take in information or focus. People with ADHD often find it very hard to manage their high anxiety levels and don't produce their best work in tests.

Advice for exam students with ADHD:

1 Break tasks into chunks. Seeing a huge amount of work can make you panic but tackling one smaller task at a time is easier (see page 90). Reward yourself after finishing each one.

2 Practise a relaxation technique to centre and calm you (see page 124–127).

3 Fiddling with something – such as Plasticine or Blu-Tack – helps some people concentrate. Ask an adult at school about this.

4 If you take medication (prescribed by a doctor) make sure you are stocked up. Have an appointment to review your medication well before exams so that you settle into the right dosage in time.

5 Distractibility is a particular problem so take special note of pages 80–85.

6 You will tend to rush and make careless mistakes so an adult can help you practise avoiding this. For example, practise opening the exam paper and reading the questions slowly.

CAN TECHNOLOGY HELP WITH LEARNING FOR NEURODIVERSE PEOPLE?

This list is a general starting point. Organisations specialising in your condition will give you the best detail. Think about:

▶ Apps and other software to help with spelling, typing, making a keyboard easier to use, concentration and even relaxation and sleep.

▶ Coloured plastic overlays may help with *some* forms of dyslexia. Investigate via one of the dyslexia charities.

▶ E-readers help because you can change the font, print size and background colour.

▶ Tablets increasingly do everything an e-reader can do and more (though tablets have extra distractions such as games and social media, so turn these off).

▶ Text-to-speech software that reads out what is typed.

▶ Audio recording apps. It can be incredibly useful for students to record what the teacher is saying. (Make sure you have permission to record.)

▶ Keep it simple: it's best not to have loads of different apps or devices. Find one that does the job and get into the habit of using it.

PRE-EXISTING ILLNESS

Perhaps you are dealing with an existing illness which could hold you back during exams or even mean that you can't take all your exams. If this applies to you, I trust that you are already under the care of medical professionals and have all the support they can give you. It's also likely to be important that your school understands the situation. This is such a huge subject covering so many different scenarios that I can really only say:

1 Follow the advice of your medical experts. Make sure they know that you have exams coming up and what your hopes and expectations are and can be.

2 Be kind to yourself. Be careful not to push yourself too hard.

3 Keep in touch with at least your closest friends, even if you can't do everything they are doing.

4 Enjoy every positive that life allows you.

YOUR HOME SITUATION

Some people have much tougher lives than others. Your parents might not be able to help you – though some parents also help too much and that's not perfect either. They may be going through emotional, financial or health difficulties, or don't have the education, skills or confidence that other parents have. Many young people are also caring for a parent or dealing with any number of challenges.

And there are less serious but still distracting problems, such as not having anywhere to do school work/revise, a long journey to and from school, living in a noisy household or sharing a bedroom. In fact, the number of you who have a perfect working situation at home is probably very small!

Advice for people with difficulties at home:

▶ If your parents can't support you, you need an adult who can for this short period of time. It could be another relative such as an aunt, uncle or grandparent, or a family friend, or the parents of a friend, even a teacher, tutor or school nurse. Most people like to be asked to help. This 'trusted adult' can be there for you, maybe by phone or social media, to listen to problems, make suggestions, mediate in an argument, give your parents or you a break, or with other support, big or small.

▶ Make sure your school is aware of what's happening. It might be personal but at least let them know *something* is happening, which is affecting your work. (If it's something that poses a danger or health risk to you, it's very important to tell someone.) Even if it's something where the school needn't know details, it's important to say that you're facing problems, as teachers can be much more supportive than if they just think you're not trying.

▶ Don't get into the mindset that says, 'This is awful: I can't cope and no one can help.' However bad something feels, someone can help if they know you need it.

▶ Don't shut yourself away completely. Perhaps you feel that your friends have their own worries; or that no one will understand; or that you ought to be able to cope. We *all* need people to turn to. If you feel you don't have anyone at the moment, perhaps because you don't want to reveal hidden fears or emotions or situations, there's always somewhere independent to turn. See the resources at the back of the book.

▶ Would it help if you had somewhere else to go when you needed to revise? See pages 53–61 for lots of advice about that.

★★★ **IN SHORT** ★★★

Everyone's different, whether through personality, learning differences or home situations, and some people have significant challenges. But lots of people are ready and willing to help you if you can just be brave and ask us for it.

SECTION 2
PLANNING AND PREPARATION

This is easier if you have at least two months before your main exams. If you have practice exams (mocks or prelims), you can also use this section to plan for them. If you are reading this only a short time before exams start, there are still many elements that will work for you.

KNOW WHAT EACH EXAM WILL ENTAIL

Each exam has a specific format and set of requirements and you need to know these in advance so you don't waste time working out what to do. For example, one exam might ask you to select one question from one section and three from another. Other exams might require you to answer all the questions. Knowing what to expect will save you effort and worry, though it's still always essential to read the details carefully.

TIP

Past papers are incredibly useful for this. (But make sure you know if an exam structure or syllabus has recently changed, so you don't practise something that's now outdated.) Your teacher will point you to relevant past papers.

KNOW WHAT EACH EXAM IS TESTING

This is partly about what material the exam covers. So, for
example, a history exam will cover certain periods or topics in
history. And it's partly about what skills the exam is trying to test.
For example, a history exam you might take at 16 would require
different levels of understanding from one you might take at 18,
even if the periods and topics were identical. You need to know
what material to cover and how to show that you know it.

*NOTE: Do this by asking your teacher, not going online.
Your teacher or head of department may have selected
certain options. Sometimes teachers decide to omit part
of a syllabus, as it might be better to focus on
90 per cent of the topics, not all.*

Some subjects rely on coursework or a
portfolio. Make sure you know exactly what you
have to complete and when.

MAKE A REVISION TIMETABLE

People have different ways of doing this and you need to find
what works for you. Discuss with your friends. Your teachers will
have suggestions, too. See the Appendices on pages 143–153)
for some resources for this.

How to create your revision timetable

You can do this on paper or on a computer. If on a computer,
use a spreadsheet or table function, or a template provided by
the many free online resources. You will need to alter this often,
which is why many people like to do it on a computer.

My instructions are based on a paper version but you can apply
all the same rules for your electronic one. You might in any case
like to do a rough paper one first to work out how to do it on
screen.

You will actually need two timetables: one with a smallish space for each day, to give a quick view without much detail, and a longer one showing a week to a page, offering more detail for each day.

NOTE: *If you're doing it on paper, use a light pencil at first, as you won't get it right straightaway. You might even make paper rectangles to shift around till you get it right.*

▶ Make your first chart with a space for each day from tomorrow until your last exam. If you can fit this on one page, that's ideal. Then make your second chart with a page for each week. For these weekly pages, each day should have slots of an hour or even half hour of the working day.

▶ Put each exam in the right space on both timetables.

▶ Record any deadlines for handing in coursework or assignments.

▶ Block off times when you won't be able to revise, for example because of a competition, medical appointment or family occasions.

▶ Think about what subjects take more revision and how long each needs. Then, in *pencil*, allocate sections of time per subject, finishing about a month before the first exam (or less if you don't have that time). Break the subjects up. Don't be tempted to spend a whole week on history, for example – alternate the days.

▶ For the last 4 weeks or so, allocate time for going over every subject twice, remembering that some subjects need more time than others. You can change this as you go, so don't worry if you don't know exactly how much time you'll need for each subject.

▶ Build in time off – relaxation every day and the occasional half or whole day off. Remember: you might lose time through illness, so you need to allow some spare days for that. Obviously, you don't know when you'll be ill but just keep some flexibility rather than filling every day with revision.

TIP
Alternate easier, favourite subjects with harder, least favourites. Don't leave your worst one till last. Best start with an easy one then go straight to the tough one.

You can make it as big and bright and bold as you like but keep the actual tasks in pencil, so you can alter things as you go.

Pin it up in your room, but don't put it where you can see it while in bed: your bed is for sleeping!

Now you can start to feel more in control. It might look overwhelming at first but at least you know what you're dealing with and what your targets are. Step by step, staying focused, keeping calm.

You can do this!

PRACTISING EXAM SKILLS AND SITUATIONS

At some point, teachers will give you opportunities to practise doing exams. If you have 'mock' or 'prelim' exams, this will feel almost as stressful as the real exams. It's actually helpful to view them seriously so that you can experience the level of nervousness you're likely to feel when the real ones happen.

Use mock exams to become familiar with how your body reacts under pressure. When something feels bad or goes wrong, use it as a learning point:

▶ *What could I do next time to make this better?*

▶ *What do I need some extra help with?*

▶ *Who can advise me on that particular problem?*

As well as rehearsing and preparing for the sensations of nerves, the actual skills required to perform well in the exam are important.

Here are some tips for this. You should practise thinking in these ways with every piece of homework you're given from now on:

1 Check that the instructions are what you expected. Which questions are compulsory? How many must you answer?

2 Read the questions at least once more than you think you need to. So many people – including me! – have stories to tell of how they messed up an exam by not reading a question properly.

3 Next ask yourself whether you could have misunderstood the question. Is there another way to interpret it?

4 What exactly is the question testing? What does the examiner want to get from you?

5 Read *all* the questions before choosing the one you'll start with. You might regret starting to answer one if you hadn't realised there was an even better one.

6 Make sure no pages are stuck together!

7 Calculate how long you should spend on each answer. Allow 10 minutes at the end for checking.

8 Plan your answer with a few rough notes. This will help keep you on track and make the process faster. Planning time is never wasted.

9 Answer an easier one first, to give you confidence, followed by a hard one so you know you've done the tough stuff.

Start to notice your weak points during mock exams: these will usually be your least favourite areas so be brave enough to practise them more than the easy things. Ask for help with these tricky areas if necessary and do so early.

ASKING FOR HELP EARLY

How willing you are to ask for help and how easy you find it to ask depends on personality, mood and positivity, and how easy various teachers make it. You'll find some of the advice that follows more relevant than others.

In the early stages of revision

▶ If it's a question about *what* to revise or what to expect from the exam, don't try to find out for yourself. Your teachers are the best source. *Do not delay with these questions, otherwise you could waste time.*

▶ If there's a topic you're missing notes for, *ask early*. Teachers can't always remember exactly who missed what through illness, for example.

▶ If there are a few specific things you want to know, *ask early*.

TIP

Discuss with your friends which resources they are using. And ask your teacher which they recommend, so that you ensure you find good quality resources. Note, too, that different people may find different resources more suitable for them so be prepared to try out a few so that you can find the ones that work best for you.

In later stages of revision

▶ Get together with others who are having trouble with the same thing. First, see if you can work it out together but, if you can't, send a message to the teacher that you'd like to go over it again.

▶ To get the best out of your teacher, ask for advice at a sensible time. Teachers are very busy and choosing the best moment and asking in the right way will mean you get their help. Write a note saying you're having trouble and ask for a meeting. If you have an electronic system of communicating, word your request carefully and politely: avoid bombarding them with massive questions that demand long answers. Teachers have home lives and need the evenings so don't expect answers immediately.

TIP

Remember that it's very, very unlikely
that you're the only one in the class who's
having the same difficulty, so do ask other
friends for advice, or ask the teacher
for help during class.

▶ Teachers are not psychic: they don't know you
need help unless you ask. If you're finding it
difficult to pluck up courage or you don't know
how to word your question or there's any other
reason preventing you from requesting help,
ask another adult how you can best do it.

▶ If for any reason you find it difficult to ask a relevant subject
teacher, ask your head of year or guidance teacher or the
head of department. There is someone in your school who
can get you the help you need.

ACTION!

**Make a note of what you need to ask. Use your
phone or laptop to keep a running list of things
you need to ask about.**

TIP

When you ask for help, you might forget
the answer, so write it down or ask if you
can record the answer on your phone.

When something is worrying you:

1 First, write your worry or question down.

2 Write the name of someone you could ask for help.

3 If it's not too late to contact the person today, do it. If it is too late, put the paper on the floor by your door, and ignore it untIl morning. Worrying about it won't help, but now that you have a plan for dealing with it you've done all you can do.

★★★ **IN SHORT** ★★★

Your teachers want to help you, but they don't know you need help unless you say so. Don't leave it too late. Asking for help is not a sign of weakness: it's a sensible, proactive part of learning and preparing to do your best in exams. The sooner you ask for help, the better. Even if you think it's too late, it's not: do it.

PREPARE YOUR WORK SPACES

Most people don't have complete control over where they work. But there will definitely be things you can do to make your spaces the best they can be. Notice I say 'spaces'. That's because it's good to think of more than one place. The brain loves variety: moving to a different place can kick your brain into gear and change your perspective and mood.

Here are some spaces to consider

I'll explain advantages and disadvantages and then I'll show you how you can make your choices work.

▶ Your bedroom

Advantages: you can usually have a lot of control over what happens in this space; it's probably quiet.

Disadvantages: it's where you sleep, so you might feel sleepy when working or unrelaxed when trying to sleep; you might share it with a sibling who might make it messy or noisy.

▶ Another room in your home:

Advantages: you can make it feel like a workspace so your brain focuses on work, not sleep.

Disadvantages: you may not have much control over what happens in it; you might be interrupted unless you can set rules.

▶ A friend's house:

Advantages: working with someone else can be motivating; it's not where you sleep.

Disadvantages: you could distract each other; if one of you is working better than the other, the one who is struggling could feel anxious; the same disadvantages apply as for working in another room in your house.

▶ An adult relative's house – e.g. grandparents or other relatives:

Advantages: not where you sleep; the adult can help keep you on track while also making sure you have breaks and bring you drinks or snacks to keep your energy levels up.

Disadvantages: you might lack control over the space and not be able to leave your books or stationery there.

▶ A public or school library:

Advantages: it feels like a work space; you won't be interrupted; internet access and lots of books, and a librarian who might be able to help you.

Disadvantages: you might find it distracting working with others (but you might not); the opening hours don't always suit; you have to remember to take everything you need with you.

▶ A café

Advantages: not where you sleep; people will usually not interrupt you; many people find they concentrate well in this kind of environment (see 'Noisy or quiet?' on page 56).

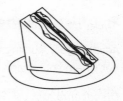

Disadvantages: obviously, noise can be a problem, but again see 'Noisy or quiet?'; you need to buy food or drink so it could be expensive!

———

Once you've worked out the options, look at what you can do to avoid the disadvantages.

ACTION!

Think about where you usually work.
What advantages and disadvantages does it have?
How could you make it better? Where else could
you sometimes choose to work?

Some things to think about:

Noisy or quiet?

The noise of other people: you'd *think* a quiet environment
would be better. Certainly, noise that you pay attention to, such
as television, an argument, an interesting conversation, will be
very distracting. But background noise *can* be helpful. Many
writers write in cafés or on trains because the noise doesn't
usually require us to focus on it.

These places *could* be distracting if someone was having
an argument or had a piercing voice but if there's a general
background buzz, it might help your concentration.

Music?: Those of you who like listening to music while
working have probably been told not to, in case it spoils your
concentration. Actually, music can *help* your concentration!

Remember brain bandwidth (pages 17–18)? Listening to
music would tend to occupy little (if it's familiar, we like
it and it's in the background) or might occupy a bit
more (if we have to concentrate on it because it's
unfamiliar or too loud, for example). But it usually
won't occupy much.

Whereas there are a couple of things that would occupy a lot of bandwidth, which can ruin your focus: being irritated by other noises in the house or negative or worrying thoughts, even relatively simple things such as 'I'm really bored and can't wait to finish this work.' Those things are very likely to spoil your concentration and workflow.

Many people find that listening to music blocks out these distractions. Music seems to make a comforting cocoon that we can retreat into and find our zone.

There is some evidence that listening to classical music might help people concentrate and take in information. However, we don't know if this applies to *all* classical music and it doesn't mean that *only* classical music would help. There's a myth that listening specifically to Mozart makes you smarter but this is not what experts believe after much research. Mozart's music might do a good job, along with much other classical music, of helping us concentrate at the time but that's all we can say.

So, if you want music and it helps you concentrate, that's fine. But note these points:

▶ It should be music you know and like.

▶ It should be music you genuinely feel *is* helping you focus. Trust your instinct and be honest about whether it's really helping.

▶ Use a playlist so you don't have to keep stopping.

▶ Listening through headphones is probably better – it helps create that cocoon and doesn't annoy others.

▶ Avoid playing music too loudly.

▶ It's important *sometimes* to work without music – in an exam you won't have it so you don't want to become dependent.

Physical comfort:

Position

Some people like to work at a desk; others on the floor, or bed, or comfy chair. It makes sense to work in a position you like. However, here are some important points:

▶ It's important that your eyes, neck, shoulders and arms are in healthy positions in relation to your keyboard, screen and mouse, or pad and pen. You can find advice online about this.

▶ For that reason, your desk chair should be adjustable. Unfortunately, these are usually not cheap. If using a non-adjustable chair, you might need to raise your screen a bit or raise your own position using a cushion. Have your computer screen exactly in front, not slightly to the side or you'll get muscle pains.

▶ Don't stay in the same position for long. Even if you have a quality chair, get up and move at least once an hour.

▶ If you sit or lie on the floor or cross-legged on your bed, you will find that this becomes uncomfortable. That discomfort will make you move, which is good!

▶ Discomfort or pain is your body telling you to move to a new position or take a break. Listen to it! If you ignore pain over a long time, it can become RSI, which stands for 'repetitive strain injury', which involves severe pain and immobility.

Other aspects:

Keep an eye on the temperature: being too cold can make it difficult to concentrate and work well. Being too hot will make you drowsy. If you can't make the room a comfortable temperature, keep warm by putting your feet on a hot water bottle, wearing fingerless gloves and an extra layer or even a dressing-gown or blanket; in hot weather, a cheap fan blowing at your bare legs or face is good. This is even more effective if you place a bowl of cool water beneath the fan.

Avoid hunger and thirst: hunger and thirst will not only make you feel uncomfortable, but they will also stop your brain working well (see pages 93–101).

AVOIDING INTERRUPTIONS

It's impossible to avoid interruptions completely but we can make them as unlikely as possible. Here are some things to try:

> In your house, whether your bedroom or another room, make an agreement that no one can disturb you at certain times. You could have a sign that you put on the door at the times when they must not disturb you. You *need* your adults' support in this.

> Make sure adults properly appreciate the importance of giving you peace and quiet to work, so that they can help keep any younger children out of the way.

> Be moderate about this. If you say no one can *ever* disturb you when your door is shut, that won't work because at some point someone will need to. Make a distinction between when you are seriously working (no interruptions except for meals),

when you are just relaxing (prefer to be left) and when you're just pottering (OK to knock).

▶ Have your phone or other social media notifications disabled. Not just silent but completely switched off (see pages 84–85). When you're seriously working, it can help to remove your phone from your work space completely. Out of sight, out of mind!

ACTION!

Make a list of all the things you could do to minimise interruptions and make your space as work-friendly as possible. Start to action all the ones you can, enlisting help if necessary.

ACCESS TO EQUIPMENT

It is really annoying to settle down to work and find that you don't have what you need. Use lists to remind yourself what you need if you are going to do your exam revision away from home. Just a couple of minutes of thinking ahead can save a lot of trouble later. Keep  your things in neat piles so they are easy to find and always take two minutes to think carefully before you head off to your revision place. (Phone off!)

STRESS BUDDIES AND REVISION PARTNERS

How can stress buddies help?

Remember that you shouldn't feel personally responsible but here are some things you might think about.

▶ Encourage buddies to take breaks, perhaps by scheduling a meet-up after a revision session.

▶ Share tips and strategies for well-being, not just for work. So, if you come across an idea that works for you, share it.

▶ Try to avoid comparisons about how much work you've each done.

▶ Be open about times *you* ask teachers or other adults for help, which can encourage others to do the same.

▶ Notice when the atmosphere in your peer group is getting too stressy and suggest that you and your stress buddies or revision partners walk away from it.

▶ Remind each other to eat enough and keep hydrated.

▶ Generally remind stress buddies to look after themselves. Many of you will be wanting to work as hard as you possibly can but people can take this too far and make themselves ill. Working too late at night or getting up extremely early, never taking social breaks, not eating properly or taking any physical exercise: these are all aspects of *not* taking care of ourselves.

▶ If you are worried about anyone's mental or physical health, and you don't feel able to speak to them directly, talking to a teacher is usually the best starting point.

YOU NEED TO KNOW SOMEONE IS LOOKING OUT FOR YOU. LOOK AROUND YOU – WHO IS IT? WHO'S ON YOUR TEAM?

Get a stress buddy

Stress buddies look out for each other and help when things feel too much. Friends usually do that anyway, but sometimes even good friends don't notice that someone is suffering inside. And it's easy for someone to be left out and ignored.

You might think you don't have time to help anyone else. It's true that your first concern should be you and you are not responsible for other people. However, helping someone else can make *you* feel good, too. It doesn't have to take lots of time. It could be a matter of just asking if the person is OK.

Stress buddies don't have to be in pairs; there could be small groups. Can some of you team up?

If you don't feel OK asking someone to be a stress buddy, show this advice to a teacher and ask if they can think of a way that everyone could be in supportive groups and look out for each other.

ACTION!

Show this section to one or two of your friends
and see if anyone would like to team up.
Think about who might feel left out and do your
best to avoid this. You might discuss the idea
with a relevant teacher who could help sort the
whole class into small groups or pairs.

Revision partners can:

▶ Keep each other on track by checking in regularly with encouraging comments and questions.

▶ Agree a schedule for each work session and know that the other person is doing similar.

▶ Take breaks together – or at the same time even if in different places.

▶ Test each other.

▶ Read out notes to each other.

▶ Discuss essay questions and how they might answer them.

▶ Even share notes. Reading someone else's notes can force you to read more conscientiously and carefully, whereas when reading your own notes you sometimes go onto automatic pilot and not take it in.

▶ Just be supportive. You're both in this together.

Find a revision partner

Your revision partner (or partners) could also be a stress buddy or they could be different people. You might have a different revision partner for different subjects.

Ideally, revision partners should be working at a similar level. You don't have to be at exactly the same level but if one of you finds things much easier, you need to be cautious. Although explaining something to someone else is one of the best ways to fix it properly in one's own mind, one person might find their confidence is lowered so it's important to be sensitive to this.

You need similar styles of organisation. It might not work well if one of you is super-organised and likes to get ahead, with immaculately-organised colour-coded filing systems, while the other has a pile of papers and no system. (Mind you, the second person might learn from the first...)

TIP

Be very open with your revision partner(s) about what you both want, what is helping and what isn't. It needs to be a genuine partnership, where both of you are helped. Agree to have a weekly check-in where you both get to say what has or hasn't worked that week.

★ ★ ★ IN SHORT ★ ★ ★

You're not alone. People want to help.
And you can help your friends, too.
You'd be helping yourself if you did.

BEST WAYS TO LEARN AND REVISE

PRACTICE AND YOUR BRAIN

You know that we get better at things when we keep practising – this is part of growth mindset, which I mentioned on pages 10–13 – but what is happening in our brain when we do this? When we learn something new, whether it's a fact or skill or idea or anything, we start to grow connections between relevant neurons (nerve cells in the brain and spinal cord).

EACH TIME WE PRACTISE, WE GROW NEW CONNECTIONS OR STRENGTHEN EXISTING ONES.

We make networks of pathways: physical networks of connections between cells, which allow electrical messages to pass more quickly and easily. After a while and more practice, these branches between cells also become insulated by a fatty substance called myelin, which helps the messages pass even more efficiently.

Without these networks, we can't be good at something. This applies equally to knowledge of facts, words and names;

concepts in maths; ideas and theories from history
or science; knowing how to use a computer
or program; and physical processes such
as playing a musical instrument, aiming a
ball into a net, bouncing a ball on your foot or
riding a bike. In fact, anything which once upon
a time you couldn't do or didn't know.

These pathways also form when we watch someone do
something. Watching a good footballer in action helps your brain
build the networks you'll use when you do that action yourself.
Perfect excuse for watching football!

This is why people say (annoyingly) 'practice makes perfect'. It's
annoying because we usually don't become perfect. But we *do*
become better.

THE MORE WE PRACTISE, THE EASIER IT IS.

However, there's a problem to look out for. We might practise
in the wrong way. Or even keep reinforcing something false,
something we hadn't understood correctly. This is why good
teaching is crucial, as well as listening to your teachers and being
open to the fact that you might have missed something. If you
find something very difficult, it could be that you're practising it
wrong or that you've missed an important point that would shed
light on the whole topic or problem. If something isn't getting
better with practice, check with a teacher to see if they can spot
what you're doing wrong.

Understanding and believing that each action reinforces networks in
your brain should empower you to keep practising – revising – giving
yourself a better chance of success. Even if you hardly notice any
improvement each day, you are getting better. I promise.

LEARNING STYLES

Theories of learning styles were popular from the 1970s until quite recently. The belief was that everyone can be categorised as a particular type of learner. Schools were encouraged to assess students so they could give each the chance to learn in their style. The best-known categorisation was **VAK: visual, auditory** or **kinesthetic (movement) learners.**

Although these different ways of learning exist and can be really helpful, categorising people as one or the other brings problems. It's much better to keep an open mind, as most people will learn better when a variety of methods are used.

You may have a feeling as to whether you learn best when you use lots of **visual** cues; such as colours and images; or **auditory** cues, such as reading aloud, or listening to someone explain; or **kinesthetic** cues, such as using your hands and body to create something physical or using rhythm to learn while walking or dancing. That's fine: go with it. But don't ignore the other methods because you'll probably do even better if you use a variety!

Become self-aware, attuned to how you learn. Yes, you have your own learning styles but they are unlikely to fit into a box.

HOW YOU LEARN BEST MIGHT CHANGE FOR DIFFERENT TYPES OF SUBJECT MATTER.

You can also think about whether you like to learn on your own or in collaboration; in peace or a buzzing atmosphere; in the morning or the afternoon; in short bursts or longer ones. Do what works for you.

GOOD NOTE-TAKING

The work you put in when taking notes will make a huge difference to how easy revision is later. Some of your notes will probably be handwritten and others will be on a computer. Some might also be sound files. That doesn't matter: it's what they're like that matters. You need your notes to do two things:

1 Be easy to access when you want to revise from them.

2 Help you understand and remember the material.

Too often, people make quite random notes which fail to achieve either or both of those aims!

Here are some guidelines to help you make really useful notes:

In your own words

Never copy and paste (unless you have been told to learn it word for word, perhaps because it's a quote). Copying is passive. Putting things in your own words forces you to understand and that helps you remember. You can't remember easily if you don't understand.

Keep it brief

The shorter the better. Include a reference to longer information if you need it later. One technique is just to write one sentence for each item – each argument, principle, fact, event, explanation.

Careful with highlighters

Highlighting is a poor learning tool. As with copying, it's passive. It doesn't properly engage your brain. What it's *good* for is marking important points for you to come back to and make notes from.

Link it

When you read or think something that connects with something else you already know, make a note of this. Connections help 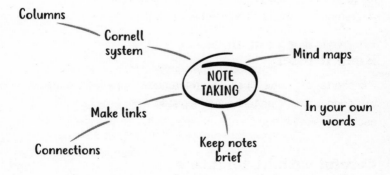 your brain understand and remember. For example, write a word or add a comment in the margin of your notes: 'Reminds me of Macbeth – guilt!' 'Stalin would have agreed!' 'Look at broccoli for fractals next time we eat it.'

Mind mapping

Lots of people find this effective. There is software but I've never found any better than pens and paper. If you haven't learnt to mind map, you'll find lots of online advice.

This allows you to make connections and have thoughts and ideas as you go. It's easy to add a note to check something later, or link one idea with another. So it's good for creating crucial understanding, before the work of revising.

Columns

Cornell system

Mind maps

NOTE TAKING

Make links

In your own words

Connections

Keep notes brief

The Cornell system

Created at Cornell University, this system works just as well in schools. (See the resources for a reference or search online.)

First, divide your page into two columns: a narrow one on the left occupying less than 1/3 of the page. That is the 'cue' column. The larger one is called 'note-taking'.

1 Write notes (in class or after reading something) in 'note-taking'.

2 Afterwards, in the cue column write questions or topics that the notes answer. For example, 'Macbeth's feelings before D's murder.'

3 Cover the note-taking column and try to answer the questions or say something about the topics. (In your head or on scrap paper.)

4 Reflect: think about what it means, whether you fully understand, how it fits what you already know.

5 Review and revise: go over it again once a week.

Organising your notes

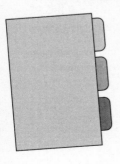

If you do this as you go, you'll be glad later! Many people find having a different coloured folder (or tab) for each subject is best.

Evernote and *One Note* are great pieces of software for organising notes on a computer. You can add links to websites, sound files, timetables. And you can access them from different devices.

Powerpoint, *Keynote* and *Prezi* are designed for presentations but work well for note-taking. You can put bullet points on each slide and use them like flashcards or imagine giving a presentation: a great way to learn.

New programs appear all the time and there's usually no cost. But be cautious about trying too many: pick one that works for you and stick with it, as searching for and testing new ones can take more time than it's worth.

At the end of every work session, take a few minutes to file your notes correctly. Then close the files. Make that part of your routine. Then it's time to relax.

TIP

Discuss with your friends how they organise notes.
Is there anything you can learn from each other?

REVISION TIPS AND TECHNIQUES

In recent years, scientists have learnt a lot about learning, which may be very different from what your parents remember. **This is a really important section and I recommend you make a list of the methods and pin it to your wall.** And this doesn't just apply to revision but all types of learning.

TIP

Quality is better than quantity. A great half hour is
better than an hour of poor focus.

Interleaving tasks

Split big tasks up and mix topics around. Supposing you have two days set aside for history: you will learn better if you spread that over *more* days, interleaving with other subjects. Or if you've decided to spend today on science, split it into different topics and go back and forth between them, 30-40 minutes at a time.

Stop before you finish

It's better to stop before finishing a topic, have a break (or a different task) and then go back to it. In the break, your brain will subconsciously process it and you'll return with fresh insights and deeper understanding.

Vary learning locations

Although it *can* be good to work in the same place (because it's easy to get into the zone) there are advantages to using different places. Your brain becomes alert in a new location. Also, if you always revise in one place, the revision becomes associated with that place; if you learn in different places, the material becomes independent of place and more secure in your brain.

You don't need many locations; just sometimes work somewhere else.

Self-testing

This is a really strong method, much better than simply re-reading.

Home-made flashcards work well. For example, in maths you could have a set of cards with mathematical formulae on; in biology, functions of different parts of the body; in history some key facts. On one side you write the question or keyword and on the back the key facts. In each subject, you have a pile that you still need to learn and a pile that you know; when you get one right it goes on the second pile, until the first pile is tiny or non-existent. Remember sometimes to re-test the second pile, though.

Pre-testing

Testing yourself before you've revised sound pointless but it's not. Suppose you're about to start revising the causes of the First World War. Before looking at your notes, you would write down (or say) what you already know; you could get some questions from past papers and try to answer them briefly. This helps because when you start reading the actual material, your brain is primed to notice what you needed to know. You are reading with a sense that you know what you're reading *for* and what you're trying to understand. That in turn helps understanding and it's much easier to remember what we understand and what makes sense.

TESTING IN ADVANCE HELPS UNDERSTANDING, WHICH HELPS MEMORY.

Spaced learning or spaced repetition

There are several theories and methods and lots of science about forgetting and remembering. In general, focus on the idea – called the 'spacing effect' – that to make something go into long-term memory and stay there, we should revise it *with increasing gaps* between sessions. Learning something all in one go is not as effective as spacing out your sessions. Spacing sessions with equal gaps is not as effective as starting with small gaps and increasing them quickly.

If you look online (and you'll find a couple of resources at the end of this book) you'll find various methods but as an example: if you learnt something one morning, look at it again that evening, then two days later, then four days after that, then ten days after that.

Or, if you only have one day in total, look at it after five minutes, then half an hour, then two hours, then the evening. If you have eight weeks before exams, you'd want to have the last revision session a few hours before, so work back from that to give yourself the right spacing.

If you have a long space of time, you still need to make sure the gap between the first few sessions is not so long that you've already forgotten. Therefore, doing your second session only a few hours or one day later is important, rather than a week later, by which time you probably won't remember it.

When you have a lot of facts to learn, flashcards are great for this because you have a box of 'well-known' and a box of 'not well-known' cards and each time you revise the material you move it as necessary.

Practising *how*, not just what

Exams are never only about what you know: they are also about how you show it. Each exam has different sorts of questions, such as long essays, paragraph answers, multiple choice. Examiners are looking for specific elements and will award marks for each.

Your first step is to know, for each subject, how examiners mark for each type of question, which your teachers will tell you.

Then practise actual answers. Just knowing how to write an essay is not the same as writing it. It might seem daunting but if you practise writing essays in the same time as you'll have in the exam, you will really benefit on the day. Work out how much time you'd have for any answer and practise writing to that timescale.

This effort will help in three ways: information retrieval improves knowledge; you won't have to waste time wondering how to answer; it's a good way of discovering what you don't know; you might find the same question in the exam.

Shrinking, shrinking, shrinking

When you start learning about something, you have lots of notes. If you still have that many notes when you're doing your final revision, it will be unmanageable. Your aim should be to shrink your notes progressively smaller and smaller, so that at the end you can fit everything onto a very small number of cards or pages.

You need lots of words at first because the words aren't in your long-term memory, but once you really understand and have revised something several times, you don't need so many words because most of them are in your head. Your final notes are just words, headings, bullets, facts or numbers to trigger your mind to produce what it knows.

WORDS, WORDS, WORDS

Napping – (not in school!)

Napping can benefit learning. If we've just learnt some material and then have a nap, that material is processed better into long-term memory. The same applies during night-time sleep.

A day-time nap should be no longer than 20 minutes, otherwise you will fall into a deeper sleep and probably wake up feeling groggy.

DON'T NAP IN THE EVENING AS IT'S TOO CLOSE TO YOUR PROPER BEDTIME AND THERE'S A STRONG RISK THAT IT WILL DISTURB YOUR HEALTHY SLEEPING PATTERNS.

Having a daytime nap won't replace any night-time sleep. You still need to sleep well at night, generally getting at least seven hours during those hours of natural sleep (see pages 106–115).

Multisensory learning

Most people find it easier to learn if they engage more than one sense. When most people are revising, they are largely using their eyes. If you mix this with hearing the words, that gives you an extra route to learning: you're engaging more brain parts.

For example:

▶ Use different colours.

▶ Record your notes, perhaps use an exaggerated voice.

▶ Use fingers to trace a word or formula you're trying to
  remember – do it large; make it in Plasticine or finger paints!

▶ Make a big poster or infographic – make it bold, funny, bright.

▶ Eat an apple while learning about the nutritional
  values of fruit, or the rules of gravity, or the history
  of farming.

▶ Walk while reading some facts you're trying to learn.

▶ Learn material to a rhythm – steps while walking or to a finger
  tapping rhythm. (Later, you'll need to practise this without the
  rhythm or you'll annoy everyone in the exam.)

Engage your curiosity

You can't be passionate about every topic and you might not feel
passionate about any. But you can kid your brain that you are
interested, and that will help you learn.

BE AN ACTIVE LEARNER, NOT PASSIVE.

Active learning:

▶ Expand your learning: find out *more*. If you've been trying to
  learn the periodic table, find out how Mendeleev dreamt it up
  in the first place. (It's fascinating!)

▶ Explain to someone else. The best way to learn is to teach.

▶ Argue the other side. Supposing history suggests that a certain person was cruel and misguided: argue the opposite. I'm not suggesting you argue the opposite in your exam: this is just to get the points clearer in your mind! Be the defence lawyer in a case where the defendant is pretty obviously guilty.

▶ Walk a mile in other shoes – what would it have felt like to be Anne Frank, Marie Curie, William Shakespeare, Nelson Mandela, Abraham Lincoln? Or their partners or children? Or dog?

▶ Turn the material you're trying to understand or remember into a story. There's something about stories that engages the human brain especially. Stories help things make sense and make them more memorable. It might be hard to turn maths formulae into a story (though you could try!) but relatively easy if you're working on history, geography, religious education or literature, and even aspects of science.

Mnemonics

Probably the oldest learning techniques involve ways to remember lists of facts or names. The simplest is where you devise your list so that the first letters spell a word or a sentence. This is called a mnemonic. (The first m is silent.)

For example, I use the word **FLOURISH** to teach eight principles of healthy brains: **F**ood, **L**iquid, **O**xygen, **U**se, **R**elaxation, **I**nterest, **S**leep and **H**appiness.

Memory houses

This is another ancient method that works well for things you have to remember in order. It takes a bit of practice. You start by visualising a place, usually a building that you know. You visualise a route around it. Then you focus your mind on placing each thing that you want to remember, one at a time, along the route through the house. In your mind, paint the pictures as vividly and obviously as possible. Take it slowly, fixing one thing at a time and going back to the start often.

This is also making use of the point I made before in 'Engage your curiosity' about turning things into a story.

Just doing this once won't be enough. As with anything we want to remember solidly, we need to keep revisiting it, so go over it again several times, spacing out your reminder sessions. See the spaced learning technique on page 75.

★ ★ ★ **IN SHORT** ★ ★ ★

There are many tried and tested learning methods so make use of all the research and choose from among these evidence-based strategies, so that you learn most easily and effectively.

CONCENTRATION, PROCRASTINATION AND DISTRACTION

We have difficulty concentrating for various reasons. Most people have days when we can't seem to focus well. Let's look at what can cause poor concentration, because if you know the cause you can choose the best solution.

▶ Tiredness or illness

▶ Boredom

▶ Working for too long without a break

▶ Hunger

▶ Emotional upset: big worries make it difficult or impossible to focus on work

▶ Screens, phones and social media

When we find it hard to concentrate, a common result is procrastination. Procrastination literally means 'putting off till tomorrow'. For whatever reason, we don't really want to do our work enough, so we're easily tempted to do something much easier and more fun, such as checking social media or sending a text message or making a cup of tea.

SOMETIMES WE EVEN FIND OURSELVES DOING SOMETHING THAT ISN'T FUN – SUCH AS TIDYING OUR BEDROOM OR REARRANGING THE BOOKS ON A SHELF – JUST TO AVOID GETTING STUCK INTO OUR WORK.

Whatever the cause of our poor concentration, there's the same result: we don't get our work done as quickly as possible; we don't allow ourselves the amount of time we need for it; and we risk not doing it so well.

On the other hand, it's worth saying that there's nothing wrong with allowing a bit of distraction in sometimes. We can't work brilliantly without a break, after all. And some people work better when they have left themselves too little time.

Only you can know whether your concentration is good, whether you're in control of your procrastination and whether you have the skills and self-control to avoid too much distraction. And for most of us, the answer to all those questions is 'No', at least most of the time!

When you have difficulty concentrating:

▶ Work out *what* is causing this and sort it if you can. Something you can see out of the window? (Close the curtain or move your chair.) An uncomfortable chair? (Try another.) Noise? (Use earplugs or music.)

▶ Is it because you are really not enjoying the work? (See 'Engage your curiosity' on page 77.)

▶ Are you actually tired and your brain just can't take any more? Have a short break, perhaps even a nap, and then try again. Or engage yourself on a totally different task.

▶ If a worry is stopping you concentrating, here are some extra tips:

 • Talk to someone, as 'a problem shared is a problem halved'. You think no one can help but you could feel so relieved.

- Set smaller targets: focusing for just 15-20 minutes could be a great achievement and will soon train your brain to push the worry aside.

- Allow times when you can focus on the worry but then push it aside while you work.

▶ Physical exercise – exercising in the morning can improve concentration all day. Can you walk to school, or part of the way?

▶ Try a change of scene.

▶ Follow advice for goal-setting on page 90 and revision schedules on page 89.

▶ Follow advice on working with screens, on page 84.

▶ Use music if it helps (see page 56).

▶ Try the Pomodoro technique. This involves setting a timer for a certain amount of time (typically 25 minutes), working hard for that period and then having a 5-minute break. More details are on page 88.

▶ Don't beat yourself up: fragile concentration is perfectly natural. Sometimes, you just need a break and to start again later.

▶ If your phone is distracting you, turn it off or put it in a different room. Whatever is happening on the phone can wait an hour or two until you can have a break. Distraction from phones is such a common problem that there's a whole section on it (see pages 84–85).

TIP

Don't say to yourself, 'I have bad concentration,' which would show an unhelpful, fixed mindset. Instead say, 'My concentration isn't good at the moment but I can fix it,' showing a healthy, growth mindset that gives you the power.

★ ★ ★ IN SHORT ★ ★ ★

Anyone can have poor concentration, for a range of different reasons, so don't beat yourself up but try to analyse why it's happening to you and take practical steps to improve your focus.

Circadian (daily) rhythms

Do you have better and worse times of the day? Do you take ages to get started? Or are you worse just after lunch? Do you work better in the morning than the evening, or the opposite? Can you learn anything from that?

I'm worse in the morning but speed up as I get close to the end of a working day. I can take a while to get going after lunch, too. What I learnt from that is that I need to start the day with a list of simple tasks to get through (emails, for example) but have a deadline when those *must* be finished. I also give myself a practical task after lunch. After that, I do the hardest stuff: writing.

TIP

Make your schedule *the evening before*, so it's there
for you when you hit your desk.

Managing distractions of screens, phones and social media

People of all ages have difficulty with procrastination caused by their devices. The problem is that our gadgets are deliciously tempting. Having them with us while we work is like having a box of chocolates beside us: we will keep tucking in. The brain's pleasure networks activate each time we look at our phones to see a notification, just as they do when we anticipate eating our favourite sweet or anything else we love. It's part of the addiction process.

An extra problem is that we do so much of our work on screens that it's often not possible to avoid them. Maybe we can hide our phone, but we're working on a computer with the internet connected. Maybe we can turn off the internet but it's too easy just to turn it on again. As a writer, working on my own with no one to tell me what to do, I struggle with self-discipline around screen-use, so I sympathise hugely. But I've also learnt how to conquer this!

So, how can we use and enjoy our screens but let them be our tools, not tyrants? I've written about this in detail and you'll find resources at the back, but here are my top tips for exam students. ('Screens' includes phones, tablets, computers, consoles.)

1. Properly recognise their tempting power. It's no good just saying, 'I'll try not to look at my phone while I'm working'

because that fails to recognise the power of the phone. We have to say, 'My phone is incredibly tempting so I must take serious steps to use it well.'

2 Have what I call '**Serious Work Sessions**'. You decide how long. During a SWS, there are certain rules you've set, alongside positive features. Here is an example of mine:

- My phone is off and out of sight. All computer windows/ programs that I'm not needing for the task are closed down.

- I have music, usually through headphones – even though I'm on my own I somehow find surround headphones better for getting into the zone.

- I might have a scented candle burning.

- I have a timer set for the amount of time I've decided.

- I have a glass of water.

- I have a schedule telling me what I need to achieve during the SWS and how long I should spend on each thing.

3 Importantly: notice how good you feel when you achieve this undistracted session.

**YOU DID IT!
YOU WORKED WELL;
YOU FELT THE BENEFITS;
YOU CAN DO IT AGAIN.**

TIP

Set SMART goals for phone/device use (see pages 90–92). For example: *'I will work for one hour without my phone in the room and with all electronic communications turned off. Then I will have a ten-minute social media reward.'*

Habit loops

Much of what we do is based on habits. Habits are useful because they mean we don't have to think in detail about everything. If you had to think carefully how to brush your hair or put socks on or make a cup of tea, it would take longer and be exhausting. You wouldn't have time to think of more important things. The habits of always putting your key on a particular hook or always putting your purse in your bag are useful because you usually won't forget them.

But habits can be negative. For example, frequently picking up our phone to see if there's a message or someone has responded to our latest social media post becomes a habit that can take time away from other necessary activities. Biting our fingernails or putting sugar in our tea or believing we need a cup of coffee first thing in the morning are other habits we might wish not to have.

WHEN A HABIT IS CAUSING A PROBLEM, WE NEED TO BREAK THE LOOP AND REPLACE IT WITH A NEW HABIT.

First, understand habit loops. A loop happens when something triggers an action, the action brings reward/pleasure and we are then more likely to respond to the same trigger with the same action, reinforcing the habit loop. After a short while, it becomes automatic and hard to resist.

Second, see how you might break the loop with a different and better action, also with a reward/pleasure but no negative result. After a while, this becomes the new habit.

If-Then strategy

A ridiculously simple but remarkably effective way of doing this is often called an if-then strategy. It helps you replace a bad habit with a more healthy or positive action. And the more times you do it the easier it gets because the new habit becomes stronger.

Here's an example: you notice that you keep being tempted to look at your phone when you're working. You notice that the trigger is that you look away from your work and see the phone and want to pick it up. That's the habit loop. So, you make yourself a new action: '**IF** I feel the urge to pick up my phone, **THEN** instead I will take a sip of water.'

If you do this several times, that becomes the new habit loop. It's not possible to say how many times you'd need to do it but each time you take the same action you strengthen the new habit.

Taking a sip of water is rewarding/pleasurable but has no ill effect. Equally, it could be, '**IF** I feel the urge to check my social media, **THEN** instead I will stand up, walk around my room and take three deep breaths.'

Crazily simple; strangely effective. *Try it !*

The Pomodoro technique

This is a simple but powerful technique to help you concentrate on a task and build your concentration. 'Pomodoro' is Italian for tomato and the technique is named after a kitchen timer shaped like a tomato. But you can use any timer or an app. The app might be an actual Pomodoro one or any free app that allows you to set periods of time for work.

If you use your phone's timer, make sure you disable notifications or put it on silent.

The technique involves deciding on a period of time – usually 25 minutes – during which you will work well. You will allow no interruptions during that time. (Some apps actually block social media: excellent!) Set the timer and start work.

Remarkably, you are extremely likely to work well for that period of time simply because you have told yourself to and the timer feels like your boss. When the timer pings, you can have five minutes' break and then start it again. You can decide in advance how many work periods you want to do each day. Some apps will keep a record for you and this feels rewarding.

Many people find that when the 25 minutes are over they want to carry on working because they are concentrating so well!

Twenty-five minutes seems to work because it's not too long but long enough to get into the zone. I think this is why quite often we want to carry on. Aiming for two work periods at a time (with the five-minute break) is a great target.

ACTION!

Find a free app or website which you can easily access to provide these timed work sessions. You need to have it ready before you need it, otherwise searching for it becomes another form of procrastination!

Schedules for each revision session

A simple schedule at the start of each revision session, including breaks, will make it easier to feel focused. You'll feel more in control. If you just put 'work on history all evening', that will be very daunting and you are likely to waste time and fail. So, decide a schedule and write it down.

You can, of course, also use the same technique for normal work sessions, not just revision.

TIPS for work schedules

▶ Build in breaks to help your brain learn better.

▶ In your breaks, have a change of scene. Physical activity is one of the best ideas, so go for a short walk. Have a snack if you're hungry and drink some water.

▶ Vary your tasks within a session.

▶ Never beat yourself up when your schedule goes wrong. Just ask yourself why: was it unrealistic? Off-day? Interruption? Once you've worked out why it went wrong, you can think how to make it better next time.

▶ Start with an easy task so you can cross it off quickly. Then tackle a difficult one.

▶ Break work into chunks and list each chunk. For example, instead of 'revise history', break that into four different tasks so you can tick each off.

SMART goal-setting

Goals must not be too difficult, or we are likely to fail. If they're too easy, we won't feel satisfied. The word people often use for a successful goal-setting technique is 'SMART'. You'll sometimes read different definitions but this is my preferred one:

Specific – 'Finish my art folder by Friday' is specific but 'work well' is too vague.

Measurable – 'Finish my art folder by Friday' is measurable; 'work well' isn't.

Achievable – If 'finishing revising history by Friday' isn't achievable, it's not smart.

Relevant – 'Buy a birthday present for Mum' may be important but it's not relevant to exams.

Time-limited – 'I won't go on social media for an hour' is time-limited but 'I won't go on social media' isn't.

New Year's resolutions fail because they're often things such as 'I will eat more healthily', 'I will drink more water', 'I will stop procrastinating', 'I will exercise more'. Not smart.

AcTION!

Write some SMART goals for your next work session. Give plenty of detail. And then write some for the next week or two. Keep them where you can see them as you're working.

Here are some suggested SMART goals:

▶ 'I will focus for one hour and not look at my phone.'

▶ 'I will stop working by 9 pm (or choose an earlier time) every evening and have an hour relaxing while I get ready for bed.'

▶ 'This evening, I will work for two lots of 25 minutes and then go for a 15-minute walk.'

▶ 'I will finish going through my science notes by Friday evening and then have Saturday off.'

TIP

Buy a cheap whiteboard and put each day's tasks on it. Include relaxation, exercise, social time and eating in your list of tasks.

★ ★ ★ IN SHORT ★ ★ ★

There are many ways to make your revision sessions really constructive: harnessing the power of practice, using certain note-taking methods followed by proven revision strategies, as well as boosting your concentration and avoiding distraction. And whenever something isn't working for you, try one of the other methods, because there are lots to choose from.

PRACTICAL ABOUT WELL-BEING

THE TABLE OF WELL-BEING

My Table of Well-being will show you just how simple and practical building well-being can be. It's a four-legged table. The legs are:

1. *Food and water*
2. *Exercise*
3. *Sleep*
4. *Relaxation*

With any four-legged table, *all* the legs need to be strong. If one breaks, the whole table collapses. Let's look at each leg in turn.

1 FOOD AND WATER

The brain is very energy-hungry and if we don't give it enough of the right fuel, it can't work well. The lead-up to exams is the worst time to restrict food or diet. You need quantity (for energy) and variety (for all the nutrients to keep brain and body in top condition). It's as important for athletes as for you.

The problem is that stress affects appetite.

1 **You might feel too nervous to eat**, so you might not get enough fuel.

2 **You might be more drawn to sugary, salty and fatty foods.** This is natural when stressed. It's OK to enjoy these foods but if you eat a lot of them rather than the full range of other foods, you risk not getting the right nutrients.

If you don't eat enough, or the right range of nutrients, you'll be low in energy and might feel dizzy, unwell and unable to focus.

My advice for healthy eating to fuel your brain doesn't involve eating anything you hate!

How to get the right foods:

1 First, understand what sorts of foods help fuel your brain well (see 'Foods to choose' right).

2 Second, select the ones you like.

3 Next, make sure they are in your house. A bit of preparation is needed and collaboration with whoever does the shopping. Some of the foods are expensive, but many are *not*.

4 Finally, remember to eat them! Take some into school on exam days so you have food to snack on. Plan ahead and act on your plan.

Foods to choose

1 A big variety – that way you have the best chance of consuming all the nutrients. No single food is enough on its own.

2 Not too much added sugar. Sugar is important and we get it naturally from lots of important foods, such as fruit, but too much *added* sugar can give us unpleasant energy spikes and dips and make us feel unwell. Some foods and drinks have more sugar than you might guess so use the lists of ingredients to guide you.

3 Include protein. Protein gives you long-lasting energy and helps you to feel full. When thinking of protein, choose from eggs, beans and pulses (e.g. lentils), avocados, nuts, fish, dairy, seeds, grains (e.g. oats and wholewheat) and chicken.

4 Not too much 'ultra-processed' food. (This is food prepared in a factory with many different ingredients that you wouldn't use at home.) Frozen or tinned food can be great, as long as it doesn't have lots of extra ingredients. For example, tinned baked beans or tinned tuna can make the basis of a good meal or snack but some brands have higher levels of sugar and salt. And there's nothing wrong with the occasional take-away for convenience but a home-cooked meal gives you more chance of a good range of nutrients.

Superfoods?

People ask if there are any superfoods that make brains work extra well. Research is mixed but dietitians emphasise that it's best to have a varied diet, not over-focus on a few items. There is positive research on Brazil nuts and blueberries, as well as certain oils such as those found in oily fish (e.g. mackerel), but not enough evidence to call them superfoods.

DON'T BUY SUPPLEMENTS OR EAT
A SILLY AMOUNT OF ONE PARTICULAR
FOOD IN THE BELIEF THAT IT WILL
MAKE YOU CLEVERER. IT WON'T!
AND IT MIGHT MEAN YOU END UP
LACKING SOMETHING ELSE.

Brain food

Have you tried my delicious Brain Cake or Brain Bars? Tasty, nutritious and fun to make. Here are the recipes! The cake freezes well or keeps for a week in an airtight container in a cool place. The bars keep for at least a week in an airtight container. Baking is also an excellent way to relax and de-stress.

Note: If you have an allergy to nuts, you would just omit them. But whether or not you have an allergy, you'll need to be careful about other people who may. Follow whatever rules your school has in place for this.

Brain Cake

INGREDIENTS

100 g softened butter or unsaturated cooking fat

75 g soft brown sugar (or caster sugar)

2 large eggs

200 g self-raising flour

1 tsp baking powder

a pinch of salt

juice and grated zest of 1 lemon

2 large or 3 small ripe bananas mashed until fairly smooth - over-ripe ones are perfect

200 g altogether – your choice from: dried cranberries/blueberries*, chopped dried apricots, raisins, flaked almonds, chopped Brazil nuts/other nuts, any seeds e.g. sunflower, any dried fruit, any nuts

2 dessertspoons linseeds (optional)

*dried cranberries and blueberries can be expensive but some places sell cheaper big bags that you might share. You can also snack on them – they keep for ages.

WHAT TO DO

1. Pre-heat oven to 160°C fan (180°C non-fan; Gas mark 4-5).

2. Grease a 900 g loaf tin and line it with baking parchment.

3. Mix the butter, sugar, eggs, flour, baking powder, salt and lemon with an electric beater until pale. Or do it by hand with a wooden spoon if you're feeling strong!

4. Gently fold the banana, linseeds and nut/seed/fruit mix into the cake mixture. Don't over-mix.

5. Immediately tip the mixture into the prepared tin.

6. Put the tin in the oven for 50-60 minutes. You can tell when the cake is ready if you put a knife into the cake and the knife comes out clean.

7. Remove from the oven and leave in its tin for 10 minutes. Turn out and leave to cool on a wire rack.

INGREDIENTS

70 g butter

4-5 dstspn golden syrup (or agave nectar or runny honey)

250 g whole oats (jumbo or porridge oats)

200 g dried fruit e.g. 120 g raisins/currants, 40 g chopped apricots and 40 g cranberries/blueberries (or other combination)

150 g seeds and chopped/flaked nuts eg a mix of any of the following: flaked almonds, sunflower seeds, pumpkin seeds, linseeds, chopped hazelnuts, and/or toasted coconut flakes

1 small ripe banana, 1 apple and 1 pear, all whizzed in a blender (or 2 bananas and 1 apple or pear)

Juice and zest of one lemon

WHAT TO DO

1. Line a baking tray with baking parchment and pre-heat oven to 170°C Fan (190°C non-fan/Gas mark 5).

2. Melt the butter and syrup until it's all liquid.

3. Put all the other ingredients into a large bowl. Pour over the butter and syrup liquid and mix well.

4. Tip into the baking tray. Press down as firmly as possible (otherwise it may end up too crumbly – but still delicious!)

5. Bake for about 35 minutes or until golden.

6. Leave to cool for around 20 minutes and then mark into slices. Then leave to cool completely before cutting properly.

The high volume of oats make these even better than the cake as a source of energy and protein. They are an excellent replacement for breakfast, if you lack appetite, and healthier than most shop-bought 'breakfast bars' which usually contain more sugar and sometimes other ingredients to increase shelf-life but not nutrition.

Ideas for foods to eat in exam time

EXAM BOOSTS *Eat before exam*	REVISION FUEL *Eat before revising*	REVISION FUEL *Eat before revising*	MEALS *Add a yogurt or glass of milk to fuel your brain well!*
dried berries	yogurt	hummus	eggs + toast
mixed seeds/nuts	fruit smoothie	cream cheese sandwich	tuna sandwich + salad
Brazil nuts	cheese + tomato sandwich	soup – eg lentil, veg	chicken sandwich + salad
Brain bar (my recipe!)	avocado dip + carrots	porridge	cheese salad
Brain cake (my recipe!)	peanut butter	cereal	chicken + pasta + salad
banana	filled wholegrain roll/bagel	cereal bar (quality)	quiche + salad
raisins + peanuts	banana cake	wholewheat pancakes and banana	baked potato + cheese or beans
mixed dried fruit	bagel + cream cheese	milk – hot or cold	salmon or tuna + rice
oatcakes + cheese	wholegrain currant bun	homemade milkshakes	beans on toast
dried apricots	raisins	oatcakes + cheese + apple	egg sandwich
homemade granola	breadsticks + dip	cottage cheese	chicken curry + rice
	fish paté	flapjack	couscous
	grapes + cheese	Marmite or vegemite sandwich	nut roast or lentil bake

ACTION!

Make a shopping list (research costs to discuss with your adults) and take responsibility for making sure you have foods ready for when you need them during exams.

TIP

When you can't eat breakfast, perhaps because of nerves and anxiety, prioritise how you *will* eat something just before exams. One of my Brain Bars would be excellent, but even a yogurt, milk or a milky tea or coffee, or homemade granola, will help you have energy for your exam and prevent that dizzy feeling.

Water – keep hydrated

Being thirsty is not only uncomfortable: it may also prevent your brain from doing its best work.

Don't obsess about the amount of water you need. Just drink enough to avoid feeling thirsty. Keep a refillable bottle of water with you and take regular sips. Aim to avoid thirstiness. You'll need more on hot days or during physical exercise.

SAY NO TO ENERGY DRINKS – THEY ARE NOT A GOOD IDEA, DESPITE THE WORD 'ENERGY'. THEY WILL MAKE YOUR BLOOD SUGAR SPIKE AND CRASH, WRECKING YOUR CONCENTRATION AND SLEEP. IT'S BEST TO AVOID FIZZY OR HIGHLY SUGARY DRINKS FOR THE SAME REASON.

If, like me, you often forget to drink, here are some tips:

▶ Put the water bottle right in front of you while working, so that you can't ignore it.

▶ Create a new habit loop by always taking a sip of water when you look out of the window or look at your phone or doodle or bite your fingernails – or anything that you do every 15-20 minutes!

TIP

If you bite your fingernails, taking a sip of water *instead* can help stop that bad habit and create a new one. Seriously.

★ ★ ★ IN SHORT ★ ★ ★

Your brain needs enough food and water and the right variety of food. Stress affects your appetite so you need special steps to keep brain and body fuelled during exam time.

EXERCISE

The next leg of the well-being table is physical exercise. There's now a mass of evidence about how exercise is good for your well-being. Exercise doesn't have to be outside but fresh air is also important for physical and mental health so do make sure you include it in your day.

Having exercise – enough to make you a bit out of breath for 20–40 minutes a day – will:

▶ Improve oxygen supply to the brain.

▶ Give your brain a chance to process material you've just learnt.

▶ Reduce stress and anxiety, particularly by lowering cortisol.

▶ Make you feel more energised when you go back to your work.

▶ Keep you physically fit and strong.

▶ Trigger chemicals called endorphins, which make you feel good.

▶ Help you feel a sense of achievement because you know that doing exercise is a good thing.

TIP
Having some daylight every day helps your circadian rhythms and therefore will help you to sleep. Try to get some daylight in the mornings by going for a brisk walk. It doesn't need to be sunny as your brain will process any daylight as being daytime by sensing it through your eyes.

We do need some sunlight on our skin, though, to help our body produce enough vitamin D. During winter months and especially in some countries, this is difficult as the sun is low or often hidden behind clouds. Do take the chance of some sunlight when you can, while obviously being careful to avoid over-exposure and sunburn. You can also get the effect of sunlight through light cloud.

What if you don't enjoy exercise? Or you feel you don't have time? Here are a few simple ideas that don't need to take much time and which non-sporty types can enjoy.

Activities that only take half an hour or less:

▶ Think of a beautiful place nearby: park, beach, hill, field, wood. Go and spend half an hour there, wandering, taking in the beauty. During that trip, include some brisk walking – perhaps on your way there or getting off a bus early.

▶ Dance to music in your bedroom where no one can see – or hear, if you use headphones!

▶ Start the day with a brisk half-hour walk or 20-minute jog.

▶ Earn the respect of your adults by doing some housework!

▶ If you live by the sea, walk fast along the beach. Walking on sand takes extra effort so you can do it for a shorter time. Result! (Stay safe.)

▶ When you are trying to learn revision notes (rather than writing them) do it while walking. The movement and rhythm can help you focus.

▶ Play Frisbee with friends.

▶ Walk a dog – if you don't have one, borrow one!

TIP

On days when you don't do some strenuous exercise, at least go out for some fresh air. Just walking a few metres and breathing in the outside air will help boost your oxygen levels and mood.

Things that take longer but could be great fun:

1 Plan a long walk (or cycle) with friends. Take a picnic and make a half-day of it. (Take sensible precautions and tell adults where you're going.)

2 Do you have a tourist site near you that involves a tower that people can climb inside? Stairs are incredible exercise and the view from the top is awe-inspiring!

3 Go geo-caching one weekend.

4 With friends, organise a fun sports day with light-hearted races you'll remember from when you were younger: egg and spoon, obstacle etc.

5 Go bowling.

AcTION!

Think of physical activities you enjoy; write them on a small card. Each day, pick two and stick them to your bedroom door or somewhere you'll see them. Set the goal of doing both things that day.

TIP

Don't exercise too vigorously in the evening and certainly not in the two hours before bed as it can interfere with sleep. Gentle stretching is good, but nothing that makes you out of breath. Strenuous exercise is better earlier in the morning or afternoon.

Important note: *some people become obsessed by exercising. It can be part of a dangerous eating disorder. If you exercise, you must replace energy you've used with nutritious food. If you find you're doing more and more exercise, using it to burn off food you've eaten, please seek help. Eating disorders are always better treated early.*

★★★ IN SHORT ★★★

Exercise doesn't only improve your physical strength and health but also your mental health and your brain's ability to learn. Build it into every day but don't exhaust yourself.

 SLEEP

Although everyone's sleep needs are different, you will function and feel better if you can get enough of it. But what is 'enough'? Scientists say that most adults need on average eight hours and most teenagers need on average just over nine.

Please now forget that, for three reasons: *first*, it's only an average and you might not be average; *second*, most people can be healthy on a bit less; and *third*, worrying about the hours you need is likely to make you too worried to sleep!

So, no panicking about sleep. Just follow my straightforward, sensible guidelines. If you have bad sleep habits, it will be a few days before you notice a change but keep going and you will.

I have two sets of advice. General guidelines for people of any age who want better sleep and special advice for nights when sleep is a particular problem.

General guidelines for good sleep

The crucial time is the 1.5 hours before you want to switch your light off: the winding-down time.

> Plan ahead. Decide what time you want to fall asleep and make sure all work and stress is dealt with 1.5 hours before, so you can wind down.

> Create a *routine* for the winding-down time. The brain loves a routine. Choose 4-6 things from the list of 'Good for winding-down' and do them in the same order every night. *Always start with the first two on the list* but after that choose your routine.

Good for winding-down:

▶ Turn off screens.

▶ Close curtains and switch off bright lights; a dim bedside lamp is fine.

▶ Get things ready for morning.

▶ Put work away.

▶ Get into sleep clothes.

▶ Listen to calming music.

▶ Have a small snack or milky drink if you're feeling hungry.

▶ Drink a herbal tea.

▶ Use lavender oil – in a bath/shower or on your pillow.

▶ Burn a scented candle/oil burner.

▶ Do some gentle stretching or yoga.

   ▶ Write your diary.

   ▶ Have a warm bath or shower; wash face; clean teeth.

   ▶ Read for pleasure.

▶ Be the right temperature – not too hot or cold.

Avoid these during your winding-down time:

▶ Caffeine (normal tea, coffee, cola etc)

▶ Backlit screens (TV, computers, phones, electronic games)

▶ Internet/social media

▶ Stress (e.g. arguments –sometimes hard to avoid, I know, but do your best)

▶ Loud, fast music

▶ Exercise that raises your heart rate

▶ A large meal

▶ Being too hot or too cold

Make a list of things you need to do or take to school in the morning. A list means you don't have to use brain-power trying to remember.

Catching up at the weekend helps a bit but if you stay in bed *too* late you'll disturb your body clock and suffer the same as jet-lag – not good!

WHY is it important to switch screens off before bedtime?

Most screens emit light which our brain interprets as daylight, so the sleep hormone, melatonin, doesn't switch on and we don't feel sleepy. But also – and in my opinion more importantly – screens typically bring messages or information that aren't relaxing. They might be annoying or exciting or anxiety-raising but rarely relaxing. This hinders sleep.

TIP
for a noisy room

Earplugs are a good and cheap solution. They don't block all sound so you should hear your alarm clock but a) experiment on a few days when that doesn't matter and b) make sure an adult knows you're wearing earplugs in case they need to wake you.

What about when sleep just won't come?

Don't worry: if you have an exam the next day, adrenaline will keep you alert. But lying awake for hours is a horrible feeling and can make people feel panicky, so you need tools in case that happens. These tips will work for all ages and are not specific to exams, though I've included a couple of exam-related aspects.

Tips for problem nights

1 Tell yourself: 'This is nothing to worry about – adrenaline will keep my brain on top form for an exam and people cope fine after a bad night.'

2 Stop trying to sleep. Focus on two things: slowing your breathing (see page 125 for belly-breathing) and diverting your mind on to something positive (see 'Calming your mind for sleep', below).

3 Don't look at your clock. It's not going to help.

4 If you have been trying for a time that feels too long and sleep seems nowhere near, get up and do something else. Read, do a puzzle, make a cup of herbal tea or a milky drink, listen to music with headphones: really anything apart from working, going online or playing a fast-paced computer game.

Calming your mind for sleep

A racing mind is the main thing that stops sleep. This can be excitement after a big event or, more commonly, worry about something ahead. Things usually feel far more negative and scary at night.
Many people find themselves spiralling into an extremely unlikely – even impossible – imaginary scenario, and this doesn't help at all. And almost no problem can be solved by worrying about it late at night, so the worrying is generally pointless. You won't make good decisions anyway.

The trouble is, 'don't worry' is useless advice because if you knew how to do that you'd have done it yourself. Luckily, I have a strategy!

I call it 'building your dream world'. This will work easily for most people but if you have difficulty visualising things you'll need extra help, and I have that extra help, too.

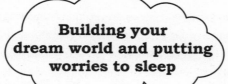

Building your dream world and putting worries to sleep

First, choose your dream: a place, real or imaginary, or a situation. It could be a desert island, zoo, jungle paradise, ship, foreign country. Or it could be based on a situation: you've won the lottery; inherited a mansion in a mysterious stranger's will; foiled a burglary; been shipwrecked with a group of friends; saved a life; won a sporting prize; performed the lead in a musical.

Second, build detail. As much and whatever you like. And revisit this every night when you're trying to get to sleep, adding or changing whatever you want.

That's all. You just keep your mind in this place or situation, building the details, enjoying the pleasure or excitement. It's like a dream where you can control everything. And, before you know it, you're asleep.

You may actually dream about it!

If you need extra help

Perhaps you find it difficult to visualise or build a story in your head. Some people do.

Here are some tips to make it easier:

1 Rather than trying to picture visual details, focus on what *happens* in your story and how that makes you feel.

2 If you find creating stories difficult, think about your dream holiday idea, or an amazing treehouse in the woods, or a hideaway up a mountain. How will you get there, what will you take, what do you need to plan? Nothing needs to happen except that you are there.

3 Think of a story you read or heard in a book. Base your dream story on that.

4 Think of something exciting in the news (positive stories, not tragedies).

5 You're in charge of your school for a week – what changes would you make?

6 Create an imaginary enterprise or charity idea for a school project.

7 If you could become famous by inventing something, what would it be?

8 If you had millions of dollars, what would you do with it?

9 If you had a superpower, what would it be?

10 If you had three wishes, what would they be? (You can't wish for more wishes ...)

What these things do is shift your focus away from the worry and on to something that will slow your mind down and make you ready for sleep. You can revisit the same idea if you want to next time you're trying to sleep.

TIP

Count slowly backwards from 100. Each time your thoughts go back to the worry, gently pull them back to the numbers.

IF NOTHING WORKS TONIGHT, SAY TO YOURSELF: 'NEVER MIND: I'LL SURVIVE AND TOMORROW NIGHT I'LL BE BEAUTIFULLY TIRED AND WILL FALL ASLEEP QUICKLY.'

What about medication?

Never take any medication unless prescribed by a medical practitioner who knows you, your age and history. Never take any medication prescribed for someone else. Never buy medication over the internet.

Occasionally, a doctor might prescribe something but this would be very carefully monitored as there's a high risk of becoming dependent.

What about herbal remedies?

Many herbal remedies are quite strong – it's why they can work. If they work, there's a risk of you becoming psychologically dependent and you don't want that.

Don't treat them lightly: they are drugs, just herbal ones. Not only can you still become dependent on them but they can also have side effects or react with other medicines you might be taking. For example, valerian, a very common ingredient in herbal sleeping remedies, can react with antihistamines, which many people take for hay fever, eczema or asthma.

If you are considering buying one of them, do follow these rules:

▶ Discuss with a pharmacist and follow their advice. Be honest in your answers about your health and existing medications.

▶ Only buy from a pharmacy or high-street health food shop.

▶ Follow the correct dosage for your age.

▶ If the instructions say not to use for longer than a certain amount of time, obey this.

What about melatonin?

Occasionally, a doctor will prescribe melatonin but only in certain situations. Different countries have different guidance and in some countries it's possible to get melatonin without going to a doctor: this doesn't make it safe or a good idea! Melatonin is not relevant for sleep problems associated with stress, which is what you have before exams. *Never* go down this route without your doctor's advice.

What about other therapies?

If performed by an experienced practitioner, you might be helped by CBT (a well-established talking therapy that tackles anxiety and negative behaviours), mindfulness or hypnotherapy. Ask at your doctor's surgery for advice and recommendations. Do this long before exams, as it's not a short fix. Always use registered practitioners, ideally people who have been recommended.

4 RELAXATION

Relaxation is the part of well-being that people most often ignore, especially in the lead up to exams. You're too busy, right? You'll wait till after the exams and then relax, right? You should wait till you feel you 'deserve' it, right? Wrong.

IF YOU BUILD RELAXATION INTO EVERY DAY, YOU WILL PERFORM BETTER.

It's not a luxury but a strategy for a healthy brain. If you don't build relaxation into your schedule, you risk three problems:

1 An overload of 'preoccupation'– your brain is trying to focus too much and for too long and in the end it won't be able to.

2 Poor sleep quality and quantity.

3 A build-up of the stress chemical, cortisol, leading to many negative effects on health, well-being and performance.

Repeat after me: **'relaxation is not a luxury'**. As your coach, I need you to build relaxation into your day, even the day before exams!

Let's get practical. It's not enough to say, 'Yeah, yeah, I can do that.' You need to plan. When will this relaxation time be and what will be in it? Relaxation is essential for good well-being.

When?

You could do half an hour twice a day: perhaps once before sleep and once at another point in the day. Plus a number of ten-minute breaks scattered throughout the day, breaks where you deliberately do something relaxing.

But you could often combine it with something else. For example, when I garden, I'm relaxing *and* doing useful gardening. Your walk home from school could be relaxing if you treat it in the right way, perhaps by making yourself appreciate the gardens you pass, or using the time for thinking about a positive project or listening to relaxing music. Going for a walk or swim is relaxing *and* exercising. Baking a cake is relaxing *and* productive.

How? What?

I have three guidelines:

1 Choose anything you personally find genuinely relaxing.

2 Choose variety – so, not *only* physical activities but also mental ones, such as reading; not *only* computer games, but also face-to-face social time.

3 Choose something that will fit your exact type of stress or mindset.

Let me explain. There are two types of stress that might affect you at any point:

a) You might have physical symptoms, such as shallow breathing, racing heart, feeling tense or anxious, headache or stomach ache. You need something which tackles those symptoms, to *calm* down, *lowering* heart rate and making you feel in control.

b) Or your mind might be dominated with worries or negative thoughts. You need something to take your mind off them.

This becomes clear when you think how some activities might work for one of those situations but *not* the other.

Physical symptoms need obviously calming activities, such as:

▶ A bath

▶ Gentle music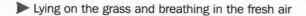

▶ A walk

▶ Lying on the grass and breathing in the fresh air

▶ Paddling in the sea

▶ Breathing exercises (see page 125)

▶ Yoga.

But none of those help with a big worry, because those activities occupy very little brain bandwidth so there's plenty left for the worry. Dealing with worry requires activities that you have to concentrate on, such as:

▶ Watching a film or video

▶ Reading an exciting book – anything that engages your mind

▶ Playing sport – any exercise involving other people (just going for a run on your own might not work for this because you could still worry)

▶ Watching sport

▶ An engaging computer game.

Some relaxing activities might actually *raise* your heart rate. Physical exercise increases your heart-rate, but is still fantastic for stress. The same might apply to things like going on a roller coaster or watching a scary or thrilling film: they might raise your heart rate, but they can help with stress because they take our mind off the problem and our heart rate calms down afterwards.

Some relaxation activities could fall into either group. Meditation and mindfulness, for example, occupy a lot of concentration when done properly, but can be calming if done in a basic way. Going for a run can fall into either category, too, because sometimes you find your mind calming down *and* you forget your worries – but at other times the worries still come. So, it sometimes depends on you and how you perform the activity. You'll know if it's working or not.

More ideas for relaxing

Think about whether you'd use them for calming or for taking your mind off a problem. People are different so the choice is always yours.

▶ Lie or sit comfortably for five minutes, slow your breathing and consciously relax all your muscles.

▶ Admire a beautiful view of nature. Research shows that looking at nature lowers heart rate and improves mood.

▶ Meet a friend for an ice cream.

▶ Watch a funny film.

▶ Draw a picture, doodle, colour in or write a poem.

▶ Lie with your eyes shut and think about your dream holiday.

▶ Spend time on a hobby.

▶ Cook something. Try my Brain Cake or Brain Bars on pages 97–98.

▶ Stroke a pet. It's been shown to slow heart rate, improve mood and even help ill people get better.

▶ Do something for someone else. Science shows that if we do something kind to help someone else, *we* benefit, too. It makes us feel good.

ACTION!

Make a poster for your bedroom wall with all the things YOU would happily spend a daily half-hour or hour on. Decorate it in any way you like. When you are feeling stressed, low or upset, you might not think of doing these things but a list in front of you acts as a reminder.

TIP

Don't cut yourself off from social life during this
time. Spending time with friends is good for you
and your mental health.

Computer gaming for relaxation

If you enjoy computer or other screen-based games, you
probably have disagreements about how long it's OK to play
for. There's a lot of research but no clear answers. One reason
is that 'computer gaming' means so many different things:
some games are violent but others not at all; some are social
and others not; although most are very
compulsive, they are not all equally so;
and, crucially, each player is different,
with anything from occasional and well-
controlled usage to excessive,
addictive behaviour.

In brief, this is what we can say:

▶ Screen-based games *can* be good relaxation because they
   can help you switch off from worries. They give your brain
   something different to do, and are fun, which can be a
   healthy break from hard work.

▶ But there can be problems, such as:

1 **If we spend a lot of time on anything, we risk over-
   using parts of our brain and under-using others.**
   We need variety to be healthy. So, although there is not
   enough evidence to say how long is 'healthy', it's certainly
   possible to spend too long on screen-based games so it
   makes sense to choose a reasonable limit. Say an hour
   a day? (And only if that doesn't prevent you getting your

work done.) In addition, you certainly should also do other relaxing things, including physical activity. That means you get a balance.

2 **Computer gaming can be stressful.** Be honest: is it genuinely making you feel good or sometimes making you irritable or frustrated? If the latter, it would be sensible and healthy to cut back.

3 **It can be addictive.** Do you find you keep playing 'one more game'? Or that you're thinking about gaming even when you're not playing? Those are signs that gaming is controlling you. You will feel better about yourself if you reduce usage.

▶ So, it's fine to play computer games sometimes, if you find them relaxing and if you're able to stop easily and do other things. But if it's negatively affecting 'any other area of your life – family, friends, physical activity, work, sleep – reduce your gaming time.

DON'T MISS OUT ON OTHER IMPORTANT HEALTHY ACTIVITIES, SUCH AS EXERCISE AND SOCIALISING FACE-TO-FACE.

Video and other computer games can be a positive part of stress relief but you need to think carefully about how they are actually making you feel and how long you are spending on them.

Reading for relaxation

Too busy to read? Too much revision? A perfect reason to give yourself some daily reading for pleasure! Lots of you love it but might feel you're way too busy. Some of you don't love it, but this might just mean you haven't yet found the book you'll love. Or maybe you just don't realise what it can do for you.

There's now lots of research about the enormous value of reading for pleasure. (You'll find references on my website.) Here are some of the benefits:

▶ Better vocab and general knowledge.

▶ Better understanding of other people (empathy).

▶ Better self-esteem – reading seems to give people better self-understanding and respect.

▶ Better school results for students who read daily for pleasure – this might be because reading improves people's knowledge, ability to read, concentration and well-being.

▶ Better mental health.

▶ Lower stress and greater feelings of well-being.

The evidence about stress led me to invent the word **readaxation**: reading with the deliberate aim of relaxing. I'm not saying reading for pleasure is the only or *best* way to relax. For a start, we need to do a variety of things, so reading on its own will not be enough. But it's *a perfect* way to relax. You're giving yourself the chance to switch your mind out of working mode and temporarily escape from negative emotions and real-world troubles. And it brings the other benefits, too.

If you're a keen reader already, you won't need a strategy: you just need permission and to believe in the value of reading for pleasure. And you have that permission and belief because I've just given them to you!

If you're not a keen reader, you need a strategy:

1 First, think of a time when you *did* enjoy reading or having something read to you. It could be stories your teachers read you; it could be when your parent or carer read to you in bed; it could be graphic novels or fantasy/adventure stories or true stories; funny stories or joke books. Perhaps you loved the Harry Potter books or stories of dragons or pirates. Perhaps you enjoyed funny, scary or gory books or books about war. Perhaps you once heard a story that affected you because it reminded you of your life?

2 From that, work out what you potentially would *like to experience from a book.* Do you most want to learn facts? Laugh? Feel scared? Do you want to escape to another world or stay in this one? Do you want to read about people like you or different people? Adventure or science or sport? True or made-up? Dragons or battles or exploding toilets?

3 Then, ask a librarian – a school librarian ideally – for ideas, based on your answers. Borrow *several* books, in case the first one doesn't work.

4 Find a comfortable, peaceful space and time when you won't be disturbed. Your bed before sleep is a good idea but it can be anywhere. My favourite is in the garden under a shady tree on a sunny day. Read! Enjoy, be proud.

5 Then *notice how you felt.* Relaxed? Excited? Calm? Proud? Satisfied? Interested? Did you get the benefits you were looking for? If you didn't, try another book. If you did, hooray – it's the beginning of a lifelong brain-boosting and relaxing activity!

READING FOR PLEASURE IS NOT A LUXURY: IT'S MEDICINE FOR THE SOUL.

ACTION!

Read to relax; read to stay mentally strong; read to know that you are improving your health. Read what you want, something you can get carried away by, something that will let you escape for a while to another world. You'll come back feeling better and more able to face exams or whatever you are dealing with.

Breathing for relaxation

We all know how to breathe, right? We wouldn't be alive if we hadn't mastered this skill. But so many people don't notice when they're *not* breathing properly – and not breathing properly is what happens when we're stressed. Correct breathing is a brilliant way to manage stress and a technique every human should learn.

Test your breathing now

Don't alter your breathing or try to relax. This is to see how you are breathing *now,* not how you should be breathing.

1 Put one hand flat on your upper chest, below your throat. Your thumb will be on one side of your throat and the fingers on the other side and you'll feel your collar bone.

2 Put the other hand flat on your stomach area, *below* your rib cage.

3 Breathe as you were before. Decide whether your upper or lower hand is moving more.

Which is it? If your upper hand is moving more, you are breathing in a stressed way. Relaxed breathing makes your abdomen relax and push your hand out.

So, when you are feeling stressed, notice your breathing. It will be shallow, with the upper chest moving more. The answer is called 'belly-breathing' because it involves focusing so your breathing moves your belly instead. There are YouTube videos which will show you how. And there's a free audio download on my website. But here's the technique in brief:

1 Sit or lie in a comfortable position. Many people find it easier if they close their eyes.

2 Place your hands loosely on the area below your rib cage.

3 Let your shoulders, upper chest and upper spine sink, loosen, slump. Focus on this for just a few seconds.

4 Focus on your breathing now. Each breath should follow approximately this pattern:

▶ In through your nose as you count to three saying 'one caterpillar, two caterpillars, three caterpillars'.

▶ Hold for two caterpillars.

▶ Breathe out for four caterpillars.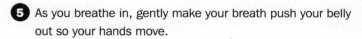

5 As you breathe in, gently make your breath push your belly out so your hands move.

6 As you breathe out, make your body sink and loosen a bit more.

7 Once you've got a rhythm, think about the muscles in your jaw and face. You have more than 40 muscles in your face and you're using many of them without noticing. See how soft and heavy and relaxed you can make your whole face. Think about each part.

8 Keep breathing like this for as long as you like. If you want to breathe a bit more slowly, that's fine. If you start to feel light-headed, return to whatever breathing feels comfortable.

IF YOU PRACTISE BELLY-BREATHING A FEW TIMES WHEN YOU'RE NOT FEELING TOO STRESSED, YOU'VE GOT AN INSTANT TECHNIQUE FOR WHEN YOU NEED IT. IT WILL ALSO HELP MAKE YOUR MIND AND BODY READY FOR SLEEP.

There's another technique called 'finger-breathing' which I've put in the next point about panic, because it's even simpler and quicker than belly-breathing, so it's great for emergencies.

Anti-panic strategy

Anyone can feel panicky occasionally. Some people may also have a full-blown panic attack, which is more unpleasant. It's also rarer. If you've had one, you might never have another, but some people are prone to them. In 'normal' panic, you feel sweaty and very anxious; your heart and mind race; you feel you can't cope; you may underperform on your task. This is a natural (though unpleasant) response to too much stress and you'll usually recover quickly.

An actual panic attack may make you think you're going to die. (You're not.) Your heart races and your breathing becomes quick and shallow; you may feel dizzy or faint; you may have a feeling of terror and want to escape from the room; you may indeed run away, ignoring your own safety or what other people might be thinking. It is not so easy to deal with a panic attack and you may need help from a good friend or an adult who can take control and help you calm down.

When panic clutches you, whether minor or major, you need an instant strategy to calm down the chemicals and symptoms. As panic stops you thinking straight, someone else may have to remind you what to do.

_____

WHEN YOU FEEL PANICKY OR WORRY THAT YOU ARE ABOUT TO HAVE A PANIC ATTACK, THE SOLUTION BEGINS WITH CONTROLLING AND ALTERING YOUR BREATHING AND, THROUGH THAT, YOUR HEART RATE.

_____

You already have the technique of belly-breathing. This next strategy is five-finger-breathing, a great emergency technique which can help anyone. You will also find YouTube videos on this.

Five-finger-breathing

1 Hold out one hand with fingers and thumb spread wide. Touch your other forefinger to the side of your wrist, below your thumb.

2 As you breathe in slowly, move the finger up to the tip of your thumb. Hold it for a couple of seconds.

3 As you breathe out, move your finger down the other side of your thumb to the dip. Hold for a couple of seconds.

4 Breathe in slowly again, moving your finger to the tip of the first finger; hold it; and breathe out while moving your finger down the other side.

5 Do this with each finger. Experiment with how slowly you want to breathe and therefore how slowly you move.

6 Do the same thing going back to where you started.

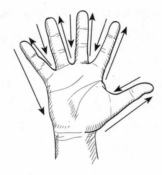

Note: *in the middle of a panic attack, you may not be able to do this on your own. You will probably not be able to think straight enough. You need someone who recognises what is happening and can help talk you down from your extreme level of stress, gently helping you focus on breathing and on a strong positive thought, such as 'I can manage this; everything will be OK in a minute.' It would be a good idea to inform a few trusted friends and teachers that this might happen to you and that they can help you do this exercise until you are feeling better.*

If you have ever had a panic attack or you are worried about having one, talk to an adult about it. Panic attacks are not dangerous but they are horrible. There are ways to deal with them and prevent them. People who have panic attacks tend to have higher anxiety levels than others and may need extra help dealing with stress.

★ ★ ★ IN SHORT ★ ★ ★

Stress is natural and healthy, helping us perform under pressure. But there are significant downsides if we don't control it. Daily relaxation and learning a relaxation and anti-panic strategy are crucial, so that stress is not an enemy.

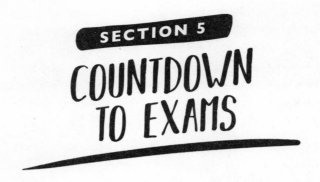

SECTION 5

COUNTDOWN TO EXAMS

You've followed my coaching programme and you're as prepared as possible. Yes, I know you're nervous and sometimes you don't think you're ready – that's normal and even healthy, as it will keep you on your toes. So, what now? How about some time-specific actions to make sure you get to – and through – exams in a state of peak fitness and readiness?

Perhaps you have come across this book recently so you haven't had time to follow all the advice. This section will help you, too, as it extracts the key points.

Some of you might find this too structured for the way you work. Or you might have a better system of your own.

You must do what works for you and makes sense for you.

If you'd like to be able to follow this countdown plan but you need help, discuss with an adult or a friend. Sometimes it just requires another pair of eyes.

Even if you don't follow my structure exactly, being organised in this sort of way will really help you and you will find lots of helpful tips on the next pages.

STAGE ONE: BEFORE THE START OF THE LAST SCHOOL HOLIDAY BEFORE EXAMS

This is probably your last chance to speak to a teacher before exams. Here's my advice:

1 Go through your official exam timetable (not the personal revision ones you made yourself) and make sure you know what each exam will require and how the questions will be structured. Talk it through with an organised friend and check you both agree. If unsure, ask a teacher.

2 Make sure you have all the notes and books you need for every subject at home.

3 Your notes for each subject should be well-organised by now, with headings, bullet points, and whatever system you use to make it easy to find what you're looking for and learn systematically.

4 Spend time working out what is still needed for each subject. Go through your notes, identifying problem areas. Make lists.

5 Things you'll want to test yourself on could now be on flashcards (see page 73).

STAGE TWO: THE HOLIDAY BEFORE EXAMS

You might not feel like calling it a holiday but I think you should, because it's a change from normal work and there definitely should be rest and relaxation. This period is important to your overall mental and physical health. It keeps your 'well of well-being' (see page 20) full. It's your opportunity to look after your*self* as well as get on top of your work.

Advice for this period:

1 At the start of the holiday, check the tips in this book and write down things that seem especially relevant for you and which you want to remember. The headings and subheadings have been designed to make it easy for you to locate and identify the main points without re-reading every word.

2 Update your revision timetable for the holiday. Aim to tackle every subject, some in more detail than others.

3 Look after your mental and physical health, fitting extra relaxation around the revision and putting it in your timetable.

4 Each day, start with a manageable list of what you plan to get through that day. Make sure goals are SMART (see page 90).

5 Keep a running list of questions you need to ask or check and use it when you have the chance, whether waiting till the first day of term or contacting an adult in advance.

6 Enjoy some fresh air every day. If there's sunlight, get a bit of that, otherwise any daylight will do.

7 If exams start soon after terms begins, make sure the right foods are in the house in good time (see pages 93–100).

8 Collaborate with revision partners (see pages 61–64).

9 See your friends.

By the end of the holiday, you want to feel that all your notes are completely in order; you've reduced them all – or almost all – to a more manageable number of pages (see 'Shrinking', on pages 75–76). You know some subjects pretty well and know which areas still need most work.

If exams start very early in the term, you might need to start Stage Three during this holiday. That's fine.

STAGE THREE: (ROUGHLY) WEEK THREE BEFORE THE FIRST EXAM

Your target for this week is that by the end all your notes are neat, shorter and ready for final revision. Work this out according to the number of subjects you have, so that by the end you have one day for each subject and 2-3 spare for setbacks.

1 Systematically work through all subjects, using re-writing, self-testing and shrinking methods (see pages 73–76).

2 Keep updating your revision timetable.

3 Remember to build a bit of relaxation into each day. This could be one long session (such as an hour playing sport) or several short ones.

4 Start building good sleep habits. Don't stay in bed too late when at home on study leave or during a holiday. Exams often start at 9 am so try to have a sleep pattern that fits with that. The best way to get more sleep is to go to bed a little earlier than usual.

5 Talk to your stress buddy and revision partners (see pages 61–64) if you have them. Careful not to compare too much, though: finding out that a friend is super-relaxed and finished ahead of time is not helpful. (And may not be true.)

STAGE FOUR: THE LAST TWO WEEKS BEFORE EXAMS

This is your last full-on revision stage.

1 Ideally you now have one day for each subject – more for some and less for others. Remember that it's better not to spend a whole day on the same subject, but to break up the material and alternate different subjects (see page 72).

2 It's quite normal to feel that some topics or subjects are going better than others. Everyone has their challenge areas.

3 You've probably got adults who are keen to help: use them for testing. Having to explain something to someone else is a really good way to help it sink into your own head.

4 Spend time during this period on some practical preparation:

• Locate or buy stationery: spare pens, pencils etc. Calculator – does it need a new battery?

• Check the right foods are in stock – and your family know not to 'borrow' them.

STAGE FIVE:
THE DAY BEFORE THE FIRST EXAM

How exciting! It's nearly over! This is what I've been coaching you for. You've worked hard and you've done all you can. OK, you might not have achieved all you wanted and perhaps not everything has gone to plan; maybe you've had illness or stress; maybe there are some topics that you feel are fragile.

It's OK. Move on. You can't change the past. Now is the time to give yourself a pep-talk and make sure you walk into that hall tomorrow with your head held high, your heart beating a little faster and your brain raring to go – or even just keen for it all to be over because, yes, it will soon be over.

YOU'VE ALMOST FINISHED THE MARATHON AND YOU CAN DEFINITELY DO THE LAST PUSH FOR THE LINE.

Here is your last day checklist:

1 Stationery and other equipment for tomorrow: in your bag? Check it.

2 Food for tomorrow: a) food you can eat for breakfast even though you might be feeling sick and b) a snack box with suitable, tasty, snackable, brain-fuelling foods.

3 Check that you know exactly when you have to be at school and exactly where. Check again.

4 Last-minute notes: do you have the final notes for tomorrow's exams, ready to read over one last time in the early evening and then in the morning?

5 Practise your belly-breathing strategy. Do it tonight to prepare for sleep, too (see page 125).

6 Have a perfect pre-bed routine tonight (see pages 106–109). If you like reading, do it – but don't read your work.

7 Set your alarm clock and ask someone else in the house to do the same.

8 You probably won't sleep brilliantly – though you might. If you don't, don't panic: adrenaline will get you through.

STAGE SIX: EACH EXAM MORNING

1 As you're getting showered and dressed, practise your belly-breathing.

2 Have something to eat and drink – you will have chosen perfect items, so you will manage, even if you eat when you get to school.

3 Leave home in good time, having checked that you have everything with you.

4 Eat some of your snack before the exam, if you feel like it.

STAGE SEVEN: IN THE EXAM ROOM

1 Avoid looking at other people. You don't want their nerves to affect you. Focus on yourself and your breathing.

2 When you're told to open or turn over the paper, take a deep breath, tell yourself one more time 'I can do this' and then do it. Centre yourself by slowly reading the instructions, even though you should be familiar with them anyway. Read deliberately, focusing on each word.

3 If there are some things you want to write straightaway on scrap paper, do this. (Use paper provided, not your own.)

4 Fill in your name and whatever else is required.

5 Now read *all the questions* before you start to answer one. Make sure you've seen each page and no page is stuck together. (Learn from my mistake in my last biology exam: I didn't realise there were more questions on the back.)

6 Answer an easier or shorter question first, to get into the swing. Then tackle a harder or longer one, because that's a big achievement.

7 Know how long you should spend on each question and try hard not to exceed this. If one is taking too long, focus on how you can move on. Getting information down is usually more important than style (unless it's a creative writing exam).

8 However much time you have left over, use every moment to keep checking your work.

9 Ignore everyone else. Don't catch anyone's eye. The fact that someone has finished means absolutely nothing at all.

AFTER EACH EXAM

1 Breathe – it's over!

2 Don't fall into the trap of all those discussions about whether people found it easy or hard or how someone answered a particular question: they might be right or wrong and it's pointless. Lots of people exaggerate through excitement or stress. Try to stay right out of it.

3 Take a break. If you can go for a walk, do. Read a magazine, chat to friends (not about exams), play a game, go for coffee or juice. Treat yourself.

4 Have something to eat.

5 If you think it went well, great. If not, keep reminding yourself that there is nothing you can do. And you might have done better than you think anyway.

6 Only after you've done all those things should you look over your notes for the next exam.

TIP

Sometimes, you'll have two exams in a row. Treat this like an extra-long race. You need to plan ahead more carefully, not just your revision but also how you'll refuel energy for the second one. Tell yourself that the first one is over now; pull the notes for the second out of your bag and scan them one more time. Eat, drink, go to the bathroom and take a couple of minutes to breathe and centre yourself. This, too, will soon be over!

DON'T CARE TOO MUCH

What if it all goes badly? Perhaps you think you've missed the grades you need for what you believe you want to do? Maybe you were ill or split up with a boyfriend/girlfriend or just panicked and it all went wrong? Are you in a panic about the rest of your life or angry with yourself?

Well, stop right now! Exams are not the most important things in the world. Nor are they the only route to success. 'Failing' an exam does not always matter. It very often ends up not mattering at all and even on the occasions when it matters it will *not* ruin your life. There are always other options.

Sit down, take some deep breaths and let me float a few ideas.

▶ You might actually have done perfectly well enough!

▶ Not getting the required grades doesn't have to stop you doing something you want. There may be a different path into the job you think you want – or a similar job that you might enjoy even more.

▶ If necessary, you can almost always retake an exam.

▶ Do you *really* know what you want to do anyway? I think it's best to keep open-minded. Why not just see what's out there? There are far, far more things you could do than you've even *heard* of.

▶ Pretty much every adult I know has failed something. In fact, failure can make us stronger. We learn as much from it as from success.

▶ Some of the most successful people in the world didn't do well at school. It's more about guts and personality (and luck) than grades.

▶ Soon, no one will ask what your exam results were.

It feels important now. And, of course, everyone wants to do the best they can and it's good to aim for that. But trust me that exams do not matter as much as you think. They are steps along a path and it's one path out of many others you can't see yet.

Sometimes, failing exams sets us on a whole new and possibly more exciting course of life. Determination, grit, ambition and guts will do more for you than exams.

★ ★ ★ IN SHORT ★ ★ ★

Planning, being organised and working hard, while also looking after your mental and physical health, are all very important in approaching exams. But sometimes things will still go wrong and, if they do, that will not define you or your life. This will soon be in the past and become your story of survival in the face of setback.

FINALLY ...

You can do it! You can't do everything – no one can – but you can do far, far more than you think, with the right mindset. That starts with this simple belief:

IF I WORK HARD, TRY HARD AND AM DETERMINED, I GIVE MYSELF THE BEST CHANCE.

We all need luck, too. Luck comes in many forms. Even having great teaching can be luck: you might have a personality clash with a teacher; one of them might have been off sick and you had a range of supply teachers doing their best but not able to give continuity. You need luck in the sense of not catching a cold, not having a relationship breakdown, not having personal stress in your life. You need luck on exam day with the right questions and nothing distracting you from doing your best.

But you can't affect any of that so don't dwell on it. Focus on all the things you can control: your effort, grit, determination.

HAVE FAITH IN YOURSELF AND BELIEVE THAT YOU CAN DO IT.

Have faith in your teachers and me – your coach – on this journey towards the best exam performance possible.

ALL YOUR HARD WORK *WILL* PAY OFF.

Even if the results don't match your dreams, you'll know you worked hard, learnt a lot and tried your hardest. And that is a huge success.

These exams will soon be behind you, while ahead of you is a life full of opportunities, excitement, ups and down and challenges, some of which you'll rise to easily and some of which will be tougher. You can grow through all of them. But remember: success in life is more about grit than grades.

Go for it and good luck!

APPENDICES

Top tips to beat exam stress

▶ Practise a relaxation technique/anti-panic strategy.

▶ Include relaxation every day – write it in your revision timetable. Make a list of what works for you.

▶ Get plenty of fresh air. A brisk walk is a very good way of thinking things through and pushes more oxygen to your brain.

▶ Prioritise sleep. Put the sleep advice in this book into practice early so you can get as many good nights as possible. But don't worry when you sometimes can't sleep.

▶ Don't compare your progress with others.

▶ If you're very anxious, find a distraction: funny video, fun with a friend, bake a cake, read a book.

▶ Stay away from other stressed-out people – it's infectious. Or make a pact that you'll all help each other stay cool.

▶ Use music: whether you want to relax or feel energised, there's music that will do it for you.

▶ Keep up your social contacts. Don't shut yourself away too much – social time is essential.

▶ Treat yourself with kindness. Including treats and time off.

▶ Keep exams in perspective: they are not the most important thing in the world.

Top tips for revision periods

▶ Make sure you know in advance how each exam is structured.

▶ Plan your revision. Plan the whole period but also plan each week at the start of the week and each day at the start of the day. Include relaxation and time off.

▶ Be super-organised with your notes: consider coloured pens and folders, tabs and sticky notes.

▶ Quality is better than quantity. A brilliant half hour is better than an hour spent with only half your mind on the task.

▶ Make a list of tasks for each day; include easy and hard ones. Start with an easy one but then go straight to the one you're dreading most.

▶ Don't bottle up your worries. Ask for help in good time. Keep a list of things to ask. Cross them off as you go – it's motivating!

▶ Review your timetable every week and adjust if necessary.

▶ Take a break at least every hour and leave your desk to do something completely different. Breathe deeply; move about; loosen your neck and shoulders.

▶ If you have any condition or situation that gives you extra pressure, ask for the necessary support early.

▶ Find brain-fuelling foods that you like and make sure you eat before work. Plan a pre-exam snack. Keep hydrated but avoid fizzy, sugary or energy drinks.

Top study tips

▶ Create (write down) your schedule for each learning session. Include some easy tasks.

▶ Take a break *before* you've finished a topic. When you come back to it, you'll be refreshed and have new insights.

▶ Always make notes in your own words – it's easily the best way to learn.

▶ Interleaving – splitting and mixing topics – helps your brain. If you have a three-hour period of time, use it for several different topics, not one subject. Switch from one task to another every 30 to 45 minutes.

▶ Self-testing is a proven technique. Use flashcards or whatever helps you test yourself.

▶ Pre-testing is also great: at the start of a revision session, test yourself so you know what you don't know.

▶ Use spaced learning: if you learn something on a Monday, go over it again the next day, then three days later, then a week later.

▶ Explain a concept to someone else – parent/carer, friend, sibling, dog.

▶ Vary locations. If you've learnt the material in your bedroom, go to the park to revise it.

▶ Learn and revise using as many different methods and senses as possible.

Top tips in an exam

▶ Read the instructions several times. Think about every word. Check it against what you were expecting.

▶ Read all the questions before you choose which one to start on.

▶ Quickly work out how long you should spend on each question. Keep an eye on your timing as you go.

▶ Answer the question you're most confident on first.

▶ Read the wording of the question again! Decide what the question is actually looking for. Try to see into the examiner's head.

▶ Jot down a few rough notes if appropriate – points to make; a maths formula you need, a quotation or a verb conjugation etc.

▶ If you're spending too long on one question, decide whether to leave it to finish at the end or finish it quickly now. Focus on getting down information that will get you points.

▶ Don't look at anyone else.

▶ Use your belly-breathing technique if you need it.

▶ At the end of each answer (especially long ones) close your eyes and take three long, gentle breaths. Channel your energy.

▶ Use every minute available to check your work. Don't leave the exam room early. You don't get extra points for finishing early.

REVISION TIMETABLE EXAMPLES AND RESOURCES

Since apps appear on the market so quickly and may also change from being free to paid-for, the best strategy if you want the best up-to-date app for a particular function is to do an internet search for 'best note-taking apps' or 'best revision apps' or whatever.

Note-taking

Lots of methods explained, with references:
https://en.wikipedia.org/wiki/Note-taking#Guided_notes

The Cornell note-taking system:
http://lsc.cornell.edu/notes.html

The Huntington Learning Center has this useful page of tips about taking notes:
https://huntingtonhelps.com/resources/blog/note-taking-strategies-for-high-school-students

Evernote and **OneNote** are great for keeping your notes in one place and you can sync across different devices. On Apple devices the **Notes** app is very versatile and easy to use.

Exam techniques

Sheffield University has quality advice which should also be good for school students:
www.sheffield.ac.uk/ssid/301/study-skills/assessment/exam-techniques

Teacher Toolkit is aimed at teachers but you can easily access the excellent tips:
www.teachertoolkit.co.uk/2017/04/25/developing-exam-techniques/

BBC Bitesize has this useful guide to the specific words used in exam questions:
www.bbc.co.uk/bitesize/guides/zwkcdmn/revision/1

Revision

Gojimo is an app with lots of free content and good reviews. It was started by a 17-year-old exam student and the content applies to both US and UK exams. www.gojimo.com

The BBC has the very well-established Bitesize resources. The main page is: www.bbc.co.uk/bitesize Revision tips here: www.bbc.co.uk/bitesize/articles/zw8qpbk

The Times Higher Education has some useful general revision advice: www.timeshighereducation.com/student/advice/5-revision-tips-help-you-ace-exam-season-plus-7-more-unusual-approaches

Tutorful publishes a free online revision guide which contains a wealth of information: https://tutorful.co.uk/guides/the-ultimate-revision-guide/revision-techniques

Anxiety, stress relief and mental health

My website has many tips for dealing with exam stress and techniques. Visit www.nicolamorgan.com and put 'exam' in the search box. My book, **The Teenage Guide to Stress**, covers all aspects of stress, including exam-related anxiety. **Positively Teenage** also has lots of advice about general well-being and keeping a positive, active mental attitude.

Two good, simple videos explaining stress or anxiety
One from the BBC's Brainsmart:
youtube.com/watch?v=hnpQrMqDoqE

And this one from the **Physiological Society**:
youtube.com/watch?v=-RZ86OB9hw4

Anxiety UK: www.anxietyuk.org.uk/get-help/anxiety-information/young-people-and-anxiety/exam-stressanxiety/

Childline offers good calming advice: www.childline.org.uk/info-advice/school-college-and-work/school-college/exam- stress/ They also have a downloadable guide for beating exam stress.

Counted breathing methods

My free audio: nicolamorgan.com/brains/free-breathingrelaxation-audio/

UK NHS: nhs.uk/conditions/stress-anxiety-depression/pages/ways-relieve-stress.aspx

4-7-8 one described here: drweil.com/drw/u/ART00521/three-breathing-exercises.html. Scroll down to the second one and there's a video, too.

The **ExamTime** website has some good tips here: www.examtime.com/gcse/revision-tips/how-to-deal-with-exam-stress/

Kids Helpine (Australia) has good basic exam stress advice: kidshelpline.com.au/teens/issues/exam-stress

The Samaritans offer lessons suggestions for schools – show this to your teachers: www.samaritans.org/how-we-can-help/schools/deal/deal-resources/coping-strategies/exam-stress-coping-strategies/

Young Minds UK: youngminds.org.uk/resources/school-resources/wellbeing-tips-for-secondary-students-during-exams/

Study International shows how to make stress positive: www.studyinternational.com/news/exam-stress-into-success/

For children in care: www.thefosteringnetwork.org.uk/exam-stress Of course, the advice is largely the same for everyone but it's important for each group of people to feel that they haven't been forgotten and children in care often have extra stresses.

Dyslexia and dyspraxia

Dystalk has lots of videos about dyslexia, dyspraxia and dyscalculia
www.dystalk.com/talks/48-helping-your-child-at-home-organisation-revision-and-exams

Technology for dyslexia:
www.dyslexia-reading-well.com/assistive-technology-for-dyslexia.html

Good ideas for helping students with dyslexia:
dyslexia-assist.org.uk/for-parents/what-can-i-do-to-help-a-teenage-child-student-revision-and-exams/

ADHD

Very Well Mind: www.verywellmind.com/exam-study-tips-20808

Revision timetable resources

Your teachers and friends will also have up-to-date suggestions but these offer some good tips and methods. A quick internet search of images for exam timetables brings up a vast number of different ones. Please ignore the ones which suggest you should be working till 11 pm – this is not healthy! It's important to make the timetable fit *you* rather than your work fit a timetable which someone else designed. So, choose one with lots of blank spaces and then fill it in how you wish.

A good guide to revision timetables on Wikihow:
www.wikihow.com/Make-a-Revision-Timetable

My own timetable guide is here, where you'll also find a downloadable template with notes on it so you can adapt it to your own requirements:

www.nicolamorgan.com/blog-archive/exams-how-to-plan-ahead-with-a-perfect-revision-plan/

The Study Gurus have many useful-looking paid resources and a free weekly time-table creation method here:
www.thestudygurus.com/wp-content/uploads/2018/07/4.-TSG-Green-Pack-Exam-Study-Timetable-mini-eBook.pdf

Young UK YouTuber Eve Bennet made this excellent video about making a revision timetable:
www.youtube.com/watch?v=PzcV4aOB8bE

And she has an Excel spreadsheet with an example of hers:
https://docs.google.com/spreadsheets/d/1nMAxnrcGYqWr9tTJyNH
B4LQ5DOtDOI-xvr2I7iMJGgc/edit#gid=0

If, as is likely, you want one that you keep on your computer rather than on paper, use spreadsheet software such as Excel. Use some of the above examples to get you started.

You could also use OneNote, using the facility for creating or adding a table. You can alter the size of the table whenever you want.

You'll find a couple of starting points on the next pages.

A WEEKLY TIMETABLE

These timings are just examples but notice that I've allowed a short break of 5–10 minutes between each work session of roughly an hour. Do always have a break to stretch your legs and relax your mind but make it the length that works for you. Create a set of timings that you feel would be good for you, your energy levels and concentration, and your family schedule.

Time	Mon	Tue	Wed	Thur	Fri	Sat	Sun
09-10.00							
10.05-11.00							
11.15-12.15							
12.20-1.10							
1.10-2.00	Lunch break: eat, relax, fresh air						
	Break: snack, relax, fresh air						
	Social, hobby or relaxing time						
	1.5 hour winding-down time before bed at						

Or you could choose a 45 minute break at 4.30 pm and then a longer one for dinner, followed by another 1–2 hours of work. But don't work late in the evening

OVERVIEW TIMETABLE

This is the sort of timetable that shows you what subjects you plan to revise each day over the whole revision period. It has less detail than the weekly one but is very helpful to give you an overview of what to cover when.

	Mon	Tue	Wed	Thur	Fri	Sat	Sun
week 1							Free pm
week 2				Free am			
week 3						Free am	
week 4					Free am		Dad's birthday
week 5		Art Free pm					Free pm
week 6		English Physics					Free pm
week 7	Maths History		English Biology		Free am		

Be flexible – pencil everything in so you can react to circumstances.

Block off a free morning or afternoon here and there – wherever you like!

INDEX

A

ADHD (attention deficit hyperactivity disorder) 27, 39–41
advantages, childhood 11–13
anxiety 6, 17, 39, 100, 102, 109, 114, 129 see also stress
autism 27, 33–36
    asking for help 34
    Asperger syndrome 33
    preparation for exams 35–36

B

brain 14
    and exercise 102–105, 143
    and practice 13, 65–66
    and relaxation 115–123
    and sleep routine 105–115
    and stress response 14–17
    brain bandwidth 17–19, 56–57, 115, 117
    eating/drinking for your brain 59, 93–101, 132, 134–136, 144
    fight, flight or freeze response 14–16
    forming new connections 65–66, 68–69
    neurodiverse brains 27–40, 117, 136–137
    see growth mindset
breathing (techniques) 124–127
    belly-breathing 125–127, 136
    five-finger breathing 126–127

C

CBT (cognitive behaviour therapy) 114

concentration

    causes of poor concentration 17, 39, 57, 80–81, 101

    how to improve concentration 34, 36, 38–40, 56–57,
        81–83, 88–92, 122

confidence, improving 9, 12, 26–27, 50

curiosity, engage your 77–78, 81

D

difficulties, specific learning 27–40

dyscalculia 29–30, 32

dysgraphia 30–31

dyslexia 27–30, 32, 40

dyspraxia 27, 32

E

exams,

    countdown plan 130–142

    developing skills for 44–50

    know exams requirements 30, 44–46, 50, 131, 144

    top tips for exams 136–141, 143–146

exercise, importance of 62, 82, 90, 102–105, 118, 121, 133, 143

    danger of overexercising 105

F

failure, learning from 7, 25, 139–140

flashcards 71, 73–74, 131, 145

food,

    importance of food/nutrition for study/stress 61–62, 93–100, 132, 134–136, 138, 144

    recipes 96–98

G

H

I

L

multisensory 38, 76–77
passive 68, 77
Pomodoro technique 68, 82, 88
spaced 74, 79, 145

M

meditation 118
memory,
    long-term 36–37, 74–76
    memory houses 79
    short-term 31, 37–38
    see also neurodiversity
mind mapping 69
mindfulness 118
mindset 9–21, 25
    fixed mindset 11, 42, 83
    growth mindset 10–11, 13, 65, 83, 141–142
mnemonics 78
motivation, struggling with 8, 23–24
music, studying to (advantages/disadvantages) 56–57, 82, 85, 143

N

napping 76, 81
nature, calming effects of 118
neurodiversity 27–40
    advice for neurodiverse exam students 30–40
neurons 65–66
note-taking 68–71, 75–76, 92, 131–133, 145–148
    shrinking 75–76, 133
nutrition *see also* food

P

R

S